IMPROVE YOUR BRIDGE MEMORY

Many bridge mistakes arise from a faulty memory, and those who learn to improve their memory will automatically improve their game. World-renowned Australian player, teacher and author, Ron Klinger, shows the way in this book.

Three sections cover different grades of expertise – beginners, intermediate and advanced. The tastiest morsels are to be found in the intermediate section where the author discusses how to remember vital principles of play, how to remember which cards are high, and how to cause memory problems for the opponents.

Bidding is by no means neglected. We are all familiar with the disasters that come about when one member of a partnership forgets the system, passing a transfer or leaving his partner to play in a cue-bid. The author shows a number of simple ways of avoiding such memory lapses.

Readers of the *Master Bridge Series* know Ron Klinger as the author of many excellent books on bidding and play. Everyone can benefit from a study of this brilliant book, for a bridge player with a trained memory cannot fail to be a better bridge player.

> 'If you're looking for something different in a bridge book, try *Improve Your Bridge Memory*. This is *not* a course of memory lessons. Rather it makes it easier to learn and remember what is important to bridge players.'
>
> *The Bridge World*

IMPROVE YOUR BRIDGE MEMORY

Ron Klinger

CASSELL
IN ASSOCIATION WITH
PETER CRAWLEY

First published in Great Britain 1984
in association with Peter Crawley
by Victor Gollancz Ltd
Fifteenth impression published 2009
in association with Peter Crawley
by Cassell
a division of the Orion Publishing Group Ltd
Orion House, 5 Upper Saint Martin's Lane
London WC2H 9EA

An Hachette Livre UK Company

A CIP catalogue record for this book is available from the British Library.

ISBN: 978 0 304 36116 8

Printed and bound in Great Britain by CPI Mackays, Chatham ME5 8TD

The Orion Publishing Group's policy is to use papers that are natural, renewable and recyclable
products and made from wood grown in sustainable forests. The logging and manufacturing
processes are expected to conform to the environmental regulations of the country of origin.

www.orionbooks.co.uk

To Gary

Contents

Foreword

Regardless of the level you have already reached at bridge, you have the capacity to do significantly better. There are many areas where your competence can be improved but none will show such lasting effects as an improvement in your bridge memory. Improvement in your declarer play, your defence or your bidding could count for nought unless accompanied by a competent memory.

Some who are saddled with a poor memory believe that they have to tolerate that handicap. Nothing could be further from the truth. No matter how poor your memory is at present or how poor you believe it is, you can increase its efficiency by at least 100%.

This book lays down guidelines for improving your mental faculties at bridge, with the emphasis placed on expanding and improving your bridge memory. It contains techniques to boost both your memory and your concentration. By simplifying the workload in routine, fundamental areas, you will be able to direct your mental energies to more important and more arduous bridge tasks and to keep up a high level of concentration.

Memory problems vary according to the level at which you are playing. The problems of the beginner who cannot remember the order of the suits bear no relation to those of the competent player who needs to know whether the 7 in a critical suit is the high card or whether perhaps the 8 is still out. Accordingly, this book is divided into three sections: the first deals with the Beginner–Novice group, the next with the Intermediate–Competent and the last with the Advanced–Expert.

The first section has been written primarily for the bridge teacher conducting classes for the absolute beginners and those who barely know how to play. Suggestions which would seem infantile to an experienced player can be valuable for the teacher of beginners. The hints are designed to speed up the learning process among those who are very raw and who find all those new concepts tough going. The teacher who can make the early memory load lighter and more enjoyable will produce more bridge players and fewer dropouts.

After you have absorbed the material relevant to your status, it will pay you to study the section again in a few months' time and then perhaps annually. As you will note, there is considerable emphasis on repetition and revision, vital in order to cement principles in your memory. By re-reading the text regularly you will eradicate any bad habits that may have crept in and embed further the knowledge you have gained.

By the time you have finished this book you will find it easier to remember many aspects of your game and as a result you will be playing better. You will be winning more often and it will be no mere coincidence that you will also be having more fun. And isn't that what this game is all about?

1984   *Ron Klinger*

Introduction: The Memory Process

MEMORY CODES

There are many books on memory codes which allow you to memorise long lists of objects, names, dates and the like. These books usually include a method for memorising the order of a pack of cards when it is called to you one card at a time with the result you can repeat the exact order immediately thereafter. You will find nothing like that in this book and you will find no special codes or association lists to learn.

While such association codes are undoubtedly valuable for various tasks, they have little relevance for bridge. There is not enough time during the bidding and play of a bridge hand to allow you to form a multitude of absurd images. The negative aspect of these methods for bridge is that you would have to build new images every few minutes, a hopeless task. As the author of one of these code books says, 'In my own case it requires at least forty-eight hours before the images fade out of my memory. This means that Card Memory can be played only once in every two days. Otherwise the images tend to become confused and one's memory is not reliable. I presume that the period necessary for the images to fade from memory will vary with individuals. Experimentation will be necessary to determine how this works in practice.'*

If a memory expert takes forty-eight hours to regroup the images from a learning code, how useless must such methods be for bridge players who have to sort out all fifty-two cards every six to seven minutes or so?

MEMORY AND CONCENTRATION

Memory is 'the faculty by which things are remembered' and concentration is 'bringing to a common focus, exclusive attention', yet the two are inextricably linked. The stronger one's concentration, the stronger will be

* p. 22, Perfecting Your Card Memory by Charles Edwards (Exposition Press, 1963).

the memory bonds laid down and the easier it will be later to remember the subject matter upon which you concentrated.

At the end of a bridge session, which hands does a competent bridge player remember best? Some players will remember all the hands of the session but nevertheless some will be more vivid than others. Those will be the ones upon which most concentration was focussed. Which do you think you would be more likely to remember, a routine 3NT or a tricky 6♣ which you made by a double squeeze?

RETENTION AND RECALL

These are the two faculties which comprise memory. Retention is the storing of information received from the senses. Recall is the ability to retrieve that information when we need it. Memory or remembering is concerned with the aspect of recalling, not with retaining. A 'bad memory' indicates an inability to recall the desired information, not that such information has not been retained.

It is believed that all information from the senses is stored and retained, an overwhelming concept. Just imagine—every bridge hand that you have ever played is stored in your little grey cells somewhere. How many of all those hands can you actually recall now?

HOW AGE AFFECTS MEMORY

We use the barest fraction of our mental capacities. There are no limits to what we can achieve with the mental resources at our disposal provided that we have the will to do so. A positive mental attitude is absolutely necessary and one of my favourite experiences concerns a lady who started in my beginner classes a few years ago and was absolutely fascinated by the game. She played regularly and feverishly and about three years after those classes she reached the final of a national selection tournament. She did not make the national team, but reaching the final itself was a colossal achievement, for when she started the beginners classes she was eighty-one!

Now that is a prime example of the right mental attitude. If you believe you are too old to do well at bridge, if you believe you are too old to improve, you are right. You will not do well, you will not improve. Not because you really are too old (nobody is), but simply because you have talked yourself into believing it.

I have heard countless players say, 'I wish I would have taken up bridge twenty years ago', 'I wish I were twenty years younger . . . then I could do well'. Such players have a loser's mentality and as long as they retain it, there is not going to be much improvement in their game. Yet they have it in their own power to adopt a winner's mentality, the 'I-can-do-it, I-know-I-can' which is vital to success in every field.

Increasing age brings on physiological handicaps but with rare exceptions, you will retain your mental capacity. Bridge has this great advantage over other competitive sports. You may become too old for certain physical activities but you are never too old for bridge and never too old to do better at it.

The history of bridge is replete with examples of players winning national and international events well into their sixties and seventies. In the 1976 World Teams Olympiad I was playing with one of my favourite partners who was in his sixties, and he played as well as any member of our team. In 1970 the World Mixed Pairs was won by Waldemar von Zedwitz who was seventy-four at the time! Just imagine that, a world champion at the age of seventy-four! Most clubs have examples of players winning club championships while in their seventies, well into their eighties and in the odd case even in their nineties.

The message should be clear. Age is no bar to success in bridge unless you choose it to be a bar. It is solely within your province whether you adopt a negative or a positive approach.

MEMORY IMPROVES WITH AGE

All the foregoing is supported by modern research into our mental faculties. An excellent little handbook summarises it perfectly:

'For far too long it has been assumed that the brain declines with age, reaching a peak between the ages of eighteen and twenty four, and deteriorating steadily from then on. This decline was held to include most mental abilities—among them recall, retention, numerical ability, creativity, alertness and vocabulary. These beliefs were supported by common sayings such as "You can't teach an old dog new tricks".*

'All of these mistaken beliefs can now be comfortably laid to rest. The research of Professor Mark Rosenzweig and others has shown that if the brain is stimulated, *no matter at what age*, it will physically grow more protuberances on each brain cell's tentacles, and that these protuberances will increase the total number of connections within the human brain.

*Or as Charles Schulz put into the mouth of Charlie Brown, 'How can I learn the New Math with an Old Math mind?'

'Apart from these scientific findings, history is dotted with great minds who showed that ability was not dependent on age; among them Gauguin, who did not really start to paint until his thirty-fifth year; Michelangelo, who was producing great works of sculpture, art and writing into his eightieth year; Haydn, who wrote some of his most beautiful music in the latter years of his life; and, more recently again, Picasso, who was producing copiously into his nineties.

'Evidence is also found in other societies in which the elders of the community were always considered to be the "Wise Men", a description which covered not only their knowledge and experience, but also their ability to use the knowledge they had.

'In the light of this, the old contention that we lose brain cells continually throughout our lives and that this causes serious mental decline fades into insignificance. Apart from the fact that we can generate new connections far more rapidly than the average loss of brain cells, it can also be shown that if we lose 10,000 brain cells a day from the time we are born, we have started with so many that the total number lost by the age of eighty would be less than three per cent'.*

Now, what could be more reassuring than that? It simply remains for you to convince yourself that whatever mental challenge exists in bridge, you are more than up to meeting and surmounting that challenge.

THE ELEMENTS OF RECALL

There are five primary principles involved in increasing the efficiency of recalling:

       (1) The 'first-in' principle
       (2) The 'last-out' principle
       (3) The 'close-encounters' principle
       (4) The 'freak-out' principle
       (5) The 'play-it-again-and-again-Sam' principle

(1) The 'first-in' principle

This states that items at the head of a list are remembered better than items further down, that you normally will recall the start of events better than the middle of events. You are more likely to be able to remember vividly your 'first date' than your tenth date.

When it comes to a bridge hand, declarer is more likely to remember the

Make The Most Of Your Mind by Tony Buzan, (Colt Books, 1977; Pan, 1981). You should read it.

opening lead than a card played at trick seven. Similarly, a defender is apt to remember what declarer does first rather than what is tackled later in the hand. Likewise, you are more likely to be able to recall the card that partner played on the very first round of a suit than the card played by partner on the third round of the same suit.

(2) The 'last-out' principle

This states the rather obvious fact that you are more likely to recall things that have happened very recently. Naturally you are more likely to remember what took place yesterday than what took place six weeks ago. You are more likely to remember the last hand of the session just completed than a hand played halfway through the session. Likewise, you are more likely to recall the hands you played tonight than those you played last week.

(3) The 'close-encounters' principle

This has to do with connections, associations and linkages. Things that have a common bond are more easily remembered than things which have no connection and no similarity. You are more likely to remember this principle itself because of its being termed the 'close-encounters' principle.

This principle has a valuable application when it comes to learning a bidding system or, for that matter, devising a new bidding system. Areas of the system which use the same principles or the same structure are the easiest to recall.

(4) The 'freak-out' principle:

Things that are wildly unusual, outstanding, weird, extraordinary, absurd, freakish or humorous will be very strongly fixed in your memory simply by virtue of being so exceptional. There are doubtless occurrences in your life which are quite vivid even though they took place many years ago.

Bridge players regularly experience this phenomenon. The results that are easily recalled are the brilliant or the dreadful. The hands that stick in your mind are the weird and the wonderful, not the routine and mundane. Which hand are you more likely to remember, 3NT making four or 3NT redoubled down four? 2♠ making or 7NT doubled making? A 4-4-3-2 hand pattern or the time you picked up a 10-card suit? A raise of 1NT to 3NT or a psychic cue bid which inhibited what would have been the killing lead? An opening bid on 13 points or an opening bid on 28 points? An overcall on 11 points or an overcall on just two jacks?

Among the hands which I know will never be forgotten is the one where my partner and I had a combined high card count of 32 points and with both

[15]

hands balanced and no major suit fit, we reached 3NT . . . and set a record by going two down with the heart suit of Q-2 opposite 5-4 proving to be no stopper when the opening leader had no hesitation in leading her 6-card suit. No doubt you have equally dramatic, never-to-be-forgotten hands.

In quite a few bridge clubs today, silent bidding is used and has many advantages, one of the more obvious being the elimination of overhearing auctions at nearby tables. When silent bidding is not used, there is a general noise level which is largely indistinct but the sounds that are almost invariably heard even though unintentionally are 'Six No-trumps', 'Seven Diamonds', 'Redouble' and the like. Why do we pick up just these bids? Because they are in the realm of the unusual. Without looking back, what is the name of this fourth principle? For the same reason as the foregoing, you are more likely to remember the present principle as the 'freak-out' principle,. because of its weird name, than if it had been called the 'principle of the unusual'.

(5) The 'play-it-again-and-again-Sam' principle

This has to do with the 3 Rs of remembering: review, revision and repetition. The more often a piece of information is repeated, the more quickly it will become absorbed and embedded in your long-term memory, from which recall is almost automatic (such as your daily vocabulary, names of family members, telephone number, range of your 1NT opening and the like). The stronger the brain pattern that is created, the swifter and easier the recall, and the more often material to be committed to memory is repeated the stronger the brain pattern that is created by this repetition.

Without casting your eyes further up, can you remember the name of this fifth principle? If you had little problem, it is because that 'again-and-again' phrase struck an unusual chord.

None of us will be surprised to learn that material that is studied over and over is more likely to be remembered than material that is brushed over just once. Of the five principles of recall, the principle of repetition is by far the most important. In many cases learning and remembering is done without conscious effort simply through countless repetition. For example, why is it that youngsters can recite the words of hundreds of pop songs without any apparent effort? Because of hundreds of repetitions without any formal attempt at learning at all. In the same way you can recall many nursery rhymes and songs from your young days by virtue of repetition, repetition, repetition . . .

Nevertheless, there are techniques which will improve your methods of revision and many of these are discussed when we come to 'System Learning' in the last two sections.

As we discuss specific areas of memory training and learning, we will highlight the above five principles and demonstrate how they can be utilised to maximise our performance.

Section One: The Early Days

IMPROVING THE MEMORY OF
BEGINNERS AND NOVICES

If you teach beginners' classes, the thought may have struck you from time to time that it is a miracle that these raw players actually do manage to learn the game. Bridge is a game of such complexity and with so many variables that it is little wonder that beginners often despair. The successful teacher will focus on the simpler aspects of the game and will avoid highlighting the difficulties. By concentrating on areas of similarity and avoiding frequent exceptions, the learning process will develop more quickly and the early memory load will be lightened.

(A) GENERAL INTRODUCTORY CLASS

If you start an absolute beginners' course with a class on bridge proper, you are likely to leave behind a stunned group, some of whom will believe the whole exercise is too difficult and will give up the course. We experimented with a number of easier introductions, at one stage using the game of 'Oh Hell' (players are dealt from 1 to 7 cards and have to state the number of tricks they expect to win). This did teach the concepts of trumps and trick-taking, but it was too far removed from bridge to be valuable in linking concepts. Today we use 'From Whist To Bridge' as the introductory class (see Appendix I for details) and the associations between whist and bridge are so close that when we come to bridge proper in the second class, we have an easy time comparing the two games and *linking the common concepts*.

(B) THE MECHANICS OF THE GAME

(1) The order of the suits:
For years I railed against the person who chose the order of the suits as CLUBS, DIAMONDS, HEARTS, SPADES, a completely random order. 'That person was not a teacher,' I thought, 'else the order would have been something like clubs, diamonds, spades, hearts, in order to separate the red and black suits.'

The novice player often sorts the hand in suit order and there is mixture of red cards in the middle of the hand, making delineation more difficult. Then one day it struck me. The bridge order is not a random order at all and today in the beginners' first class, they receive a tip which means they never forget the order of the suits.

The order is *alphabetical*, **C**lubs, **D**iamonds, **H**earts, **S**pades. By associating the order of the suits with the order of the alphabet there is no longer any risk that the order will be forgotten, since the beginner has an easy reference point, if any doubt creeps in.

(2) Where to place the cards

Beginners are all over the place when it comes to the question of where should the cards be placed after shuffling. Until they have done it plenty of times, they hesitate . . . . this side . . . that side. A bridge-teaching friend solved this and other problems very neatly by composing a bridge rhyme to suit the situation. All of us remember rhymes easily (connection), the most common memory rhymes being the alphabet itself and the perennial '30 days hath September . . .'. For the problem of placing the cards she uses:

> *If you would avoid a fight,*
> *Place the cards upon your right.*
> *If of sense you are bereft,*
> *Put them wrongly on the left.*

The same is used when it comes to teaching beginners where dummy's trumps should be positioned:

> *If you would avoid that fight,*
> *Place the trumps on dummy's right.*

(3) The scoring

There is so much in the scoring that it is not reasonable to expect beginners to memorise it all at once. However, many of the concepts can be imparted simply by the expedient of association. When explaining the idea of a 'rubber' of bridge and that a rubber is best of three games, it is an easy matter to say 'It is just like a match in tennis. A match in tennis is often the best of three sets. So a match in bridge is called a rubber and that match or rubber is best of three games.'

The analogy is easily continued and through the connection with a familiar sport, the bridge concepts are quickly assimilated. For example, 'A set in tennis is the first to score six; in bridge, it is the first side to reach 100, that wins the game. In tennis when a set ends, both sides start from scratch again, so in bridge, after a game ends, both sides start from zero again and you cannot carry forward any score from the previous game to the next one' and 'If in your tennis match, best-of-three-sets, you win the first two sets, you would not bother playing the third set, so in bridge, if you win the first two games, you have finished that rubber and would not bother playing the third game.'

Obviously it need not be tennis. Any familiar activity will suffice. When dealing with the value of the suits, 30 each for spades and hearts, 20 for diamonds and clubs, it is worthwhile associating the terms 'majors' and 'minors' at once. 'Spades and hearts are the major suits because they score more; diamonds and clubs are therefore called the minor suits.' Likewise when covering the scoring for no-trumps, rather than score no-trumps as 40 for the first and then 30 each, a simple association is 'No-trumps scores the same as the major suits, 30 per trick, except you are given 10 extra for no-trumps. Just multiply the tricks by 30, as we do for the major suits, then add 10 on at the end.'

In scoring of bonuses, the more similarities you can produce, the quicker the details will be memorised. For example, early on you would give 500 for a 2-1 rubber and 700 for a 2-0 rubber. When you come to deal with slam bonuses, you relate the 500 for a small slam not vulnerable to the rubber bonus of 500. For example, 'A slam is so valuable because the 500 points you get are like winning an extra rubber'. Likewise you can compare the grand slam bonus of 1500 vulnerable with the winning of three extra rubbers on the one deal. Again, when dealing with doubled penalties, the figure of 500 for two down doubled vulnerable or three down doubled not vulnerable should be related to the value of a rubber.

(C) THE BIDDING

Top teachers of beginners' classes make use of all five aspects of memory training when dealing with the bidding.

(1) The 'first-in' principle
It is important to concentrate at the beginning of the class on the most important aspects which you intend to cover in that session. Whatever you wish the students to recall should be briefly stated or summarised at the start of the class. Of course, you will come back to the details frequently during the session but an emphasis, even if brief, at the very outset will operate as an effective stimulus and makes use of the 'first-in' principle.

(2) The 'last-out' principle

In like manner, the session should conclude with a recapitulation of the main points of the class. A brief summary of the principles to be remembered will leave the students with the most important pieces of information uppermost in their minds.

(3) The 'close-encounters' principle

Wherever possible, the teacher links similar areas together. There are many opportunities to do this but it will naturally depend on the methods you are using and teaching. Teachers develop their own connections and associations but the following are ones that have been found helpful.

(i) The 4–3–2–1 count: It is generally recognised that the 4–3–2–1 count is not wholly accurate in that it undervalues aces (c.4.25 points) and overvalues jacks (c.0.75 points) in relative terms. Nevertheless, it would be foolish to introduce anything more complex (such as the 7–5–3–1 count) since the 4–3–2–1 has such an easy numerical connection and therefore is remembered almost instantaneously.

Likewise, the 3–2–1 shortage count is unsound when assessing the hand for an opening bid but is still used by many teachers because of its ease of assimilation and the simple numerical connection makes it easy to remember. Again, the 5–3–1 count for void-singleton-doubleton when supporting partner has a simple arithmetical association and is thus easy to remember.

(ii) Five-card majors versus four-card majors: For many years we resisted teaching five-card majors because of the problems caused by interference bidding over minor suit openings. Today most of these problems have been overcome (by negative doubles) and teaching five-card majors to beginners has a number of clear advantages.

Links can be established between opening 1♡/1♠ and opening 2♡/2♠, instead of having to explain differences and exceptions. Similarly, links can be drawn between opening the bidding and overcalling, both based on at least 5-card length, instead of having to explain the need for a five-card suit when overcalling, while contending that a four-card holding is adequate for opening. The principles in a 5-card majors system are easier to absorb and remember and hence also easier to teach.

(iii) Ranges for various bids: The sequences 1♡ : 2♡ and 1♡ : 1NT (and the like) should be linked as weak responses. They have the same range and are distinguished by the fact that one promises support, the other denies support.

If the sequences 1♠ : 3♠ and 1♠ : 2NT cover the same range,

they can also be linked by the concept of same strength but promise-support versus denial-support.

For those who teach a strong 1NT opening, a link should be made between the 1NT opening and the 3NT response, if that is the same range. Suppose, for example, you are teaching Standard American and a 1NT opening with a 16–18 range. When you come to deal with the no-trump responses, you can write up an example of a 1NT opening hand that would also qualify for a 3NT response and ask the class what the opening bid would be. Then you continue 'But if partner has opened 1 . . . , you would give a 3NT response. The 3NT response is equivalent to the 1NT opening. If you were sitting there, thinking to yourself "Oh good, I'm going to open 1NT", but then partner opens first, your thoughts would change to "Oh good, I have a 3NT response".'

Links should be made between a 2-level response and a 2-level overcall. Both require approximately the same strength. Links should be made between opener's rebids which all show minimum strength (e.g. 1♣ : 1♡, 2♣ and 1♣ : 1♡, 2♡) or which all show extra strength (e.g. 1♢ : 1♠, 3♢ or 1♢ : 1♠, 3♠). The ideas in these links can all be reinforced by the introduction of bridge maxims. Many of these exist and are very helpful. In this last area, you can use 'MINIMUM REBID, MINIMUM HAND'.

When teaching pre-emptive bids and distinguishing them from strong actions, a helpful maxim is 'SINGLE JUMP STRONG, DOUBLE JUMP WEAK'. If that is then illustrated by appropriate bidding sequences, the concepts are easily remembered.

When taught the use of Stayman 2♣, students may tend to use Stayman on unsuitable occasions. In helping them to avoid Stayman on 4-3-3-3 hands even though a 4-card major is held, the maxim 'NO SHORTAGE, NO STAYMAN' will prove an easy shortcut.

When dealing with Blackwood and the 5♣ response to 4NT as showing no ace or all four aces, students will be quick to remember this if it is called the 'ALL OR NOTHING' reply.

(4) The 'freak-out' principle
In many areas, the concept to be remembered is best put across by means of exaggeration or humour. No doubt more students remember the concept of pre-empts through George Gooden's term 'weak freaks' than the dry, technical 'pre-empts'.

Teachers who can impart knowledge with a dextrous touch of humour are likely to have a higher success rate because the humour aspect plays a strong role in the 'freak-out' principle. Even a light aside when teaching balanced hands, such as 'when partner puts the cards face up as dummy, it is dangerous to say "you are not balanced!"' creates a stronger impression of the 'balanced' versus 'unbalanced' concepts.

In each of the beginners' classes we ensure that the students play at least four hands, which have been dealt with in the first half of the class. The actual play makes a more dramatic impact than listening to rules or seeing them illustrated on the board. When possible the hands themselves should be unusual for again this will heighten the effect of the freak-out principle. Take this example from a session on pre-empts:

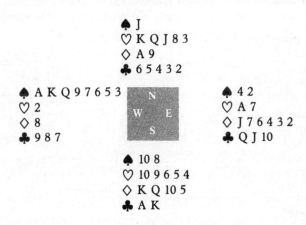

        ♠ J
        ♡ K Q J 8 3
        ◇ A 9
        ♣ 6 5 4 3 2

♠ A K Q 9 7 6 5 3   ♠ 4 2
♡ 2   ♡ A 7
◇ 8   ◇ J 7 6 4 3 2
♣ 9 8 7   ♣ Q J 10

        ♠ 10 8
        ♡ 10 9 6 5 4
        ◇ K Q 10 5
        ♣ A K

This deal is played first with West the dealer and both sides vulnerable and the recommended bidding is Four Spades by West, Pass, Pass, Pass. On the ♡ K lead, declarer should make this contract easily. The hand is then replayed with South the dealer and both sides vulnerable, when the recommended bidding would be:

SOUTH	WEST	NORTH	EAST
1 ♡	4 ♠	5 ♡	All pass

This contract also succeeds and when it is pointed out to the students how West stole the contract with the 4♠ opening before the replay in 5♡, making a game for East–West when another game is on for North–South, the message of the purpose of pre-empts hits home far more effectively because of the exceptional contrast of the results.

Some concepts are more difficult for beginners to comprehend than others. In such a case, a light-hearted approach makes the memory process easier. An area where my teacher friend had been having troubles was in discouraging beginners from showing a four-card major suit after auctions like 1♣ : 3♣ or 1◇ : 3◇. She now uses the following approach which titillates the class but is functionally successful. She says something like 'After 1♣ : 3♣ there is little point in opener showing a major since responder has denied holding a major. Since responder has not shown a major, the opener need not show one either. This is known as "The I-won't-show-you-mine-if-you-don't-show-me-yours principle".'

(5) The 'play-it-again-and-again-Sam' principle

During each class, the teacher will repeat the same principles innumerable times. However, the setting for these repetitions will change. For example, we start by stating the principle and writing it on the board (e.g. open the longest suit first, but open the higher of two five-card suits). Then follow several examples on the board and after the students give the correct answer, the teacher agrees, saying things like 'Yes, longest first' or 'Yes, with 5–5, open the higher'. Then a number of exercises from the textbook on the area allow the teacher to seek the correct answer and when given, the teacher asks 'Why?' With the students answering regularly 'Because it's the longest' or 'Because it's the higher of two five-card suits', the message sinks in. When the time comes to play the set hands, the same procedure is used. When reviewing the bidding, the teacher seeks the reason for the choice and the students in giving the reason and thus repeating the principles again and again reinforce the lesson until it is so deep it is never-to-be-forgotten (the teacher hopes).

With a revision quiz at the start of the following week's session, the review and repetition principle is again at work.

(D) THE PLAY OF THE CARDS

In our classes we concentrate on bidding in the first half and then take a 10–15 minute coffee-break before playing the set hands. The idea is to have a significant division in the session and this allows the 'first-in' principle to be at work again. At the start of the second half, principles to do with card play (leads, signals, declarer play rules, etc) can be presented briefly and then exemplified by the hands to be played (repetition).

The 'freak-out' principle is used by my rhyming teacher friend here also.

In teaching the 'lead-through-strength, lead-up-to-weakness' rule, she uses:

> *When the board is on your right,*
> *Lead the weakest thing in sight.*
> *When the board is on your left,*
> *Lead through heft.*

Corny? Perhaps, but very effective nevertheless.

She also has a very persuasive method of making sure her students lead their partner's suit. Her approach runs like this:

There are two and only two circumstances in which you are excused for not leading a suit which your partner has bid. One is when you are void in that suit . . . (pause) . . . and the other is if you have suffered cardiac arrest!

Extreme? Yes. Exaggerated? Of course, but the message comes through loud and clear.

A number of teachers try to help their students remember the suit that partner has bid or the suit that partner has led by placing it in a particular part of their hand. For example, when partner makes the lead, move all the cards in that suit to the right-hand side of your hand. At the beginner level, this practice will not be offensive and when the teacher emphasises that this must be done unobtrusively and exaggerates the action in being obvious about moving the cards, again the message hits home. The same approach (moving cards to a special part of your hand) can be usefully applied when a card is recognised to be high. A jack or ten can be seen to be high but if a few tricks have passed, beginners have trouble in recalling whether that particular card is high. This facility develops quite quickly but even intermediate players sometimes have trouble being certain later in the hand whether a low spot such as the 7 or 8 is high. By placing these high cards on, say, the left side of the hand, they can be easily recalled to be high at a later stage of the play. Until any such cards have become high, one keeps a 2 or 3 on the left side of the hand. This can also be used for cards that are the last remaining cards in the suit, the thirteenth, and so on. Again, students have to be cautioned about being unobtrusive in this movement of cards to a special part of the hand.

Memorable hands, those which have a most unusual outcome, are also helpful here in utilising the 'freak-out' principle to etch the lesson of the hand indelibly in the students' minds. This example has a stunning effect:

Dealer North
Nil vulnerable

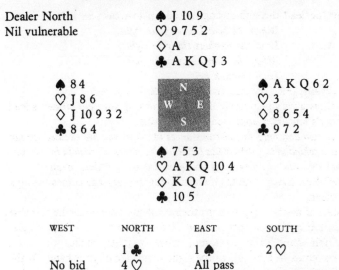

♠ J 10 9
♡ 9 7 5 2
◇ A
♣ A K Q J 3

♠ 8 4
♡ J 8 6
◇ J 10 9 3 2
♣ 8 6 4

♠ A K Q 6 2
♡ 3
◇ 8 6 5 4
♣ 9 7 2

♠ 7 5 3
♡ A K Q 10 4
◇ K Q 7
♣ 10 5

WEST	NORTH	EAST	SOUTH
	1 ♣	1 ♠	2 ♡
No bid	4 ♡	All pass	

West leads the ♠ 8 and after three rounds of spades, East continues with a fourth spade since it is clear that any switch is futile. This defeats the contract as the ♡ J is promoted. The hand is than replayed on the lead of the ◇ J. The result is that all thirteen tricks are taken. This contrast between game-one-off and a grand slam making is a powerful reinforcement of both the principle of leading partner's suit and of the necessity to overcall with a strong suit, even with little overall strength, to ensure partner makes the most advantageous opening lead.

Section Two : Easing the Struggle

TECHNIQUES FOR THE INTERMEDIATE
TO COMPETENT GROUP

(A) MEMORY METHODS FOR PROBLEMS IN THE BIDDING

Your memory problems in the bidding will differ depending on whether you are playing regularly with the one partner or you have several different partners. If you have just the one partner, you are able to agree your methods, practise them assiduously and you will not have to concern yourself with outside methods. With a suitable partner, this is the best way to progress to bigger and better achievements. Most players, however, have several partners and have to contend with different systems, different conventions and different predilections. One way to ease your burden here is to try to encourage as many of your partners as possible to play the same methods so that the area of differences will be minimised. Another is to think of your partners in terms of the methods they prefer. Thus one partner might be Jack Weak-Twos-Gerber Smith, another might be Josephine Weak-NT-Transfers-Jones, and so on. You could enter their names in such a fashion in your bridge diary, but do take care that you append the correct description (not like the new young thing who was introduced to the late John Gerber and gushed 'Oh, I've been dying to meet the 4NT-man, Mr. Gerber.').

The Close-Encounters Principle
Suppose you pick up ——

♠ A J 8 6   ♡ A 8 7 4   ◇ K Q   ♣ Q 10 9

Playing a strong no-trump, you open 1NT and partner Staymans with 2♣. What is your rebid?

Some partnerships bid 2♠, others bid 2♡, others have a bid which shows both majors (extended Stayman—see pages 32/33). There is not much between the natural replies of 2♡ or 2♠ and we would guess that most expert pairs would prefer 2♡ which has some theoretical advantages. However, there is a sound practical consideration for preferring to use 2♡ in your answer to

Stayman when you hold both majors. This makes it consistent with the general principle of bidding four-card suits 'up-the-line'. Suppose you picked up ♠ A J 8 7 ♡ Q J 3 2 ◇ 7 ♣ A Q 5 4 or ♠ K J 8 5 ♡ K 5 3 2 ◇ — ♣ A K 6 5 4. In each case you would open 1♣ and if partner produces the expected 1◇, you would continue with 1♡, not 1♠. Likewise, if you had opened 1◇ on ♠ K Q 7 6 ♡ K Q 7 6 ◇ A Q J 7 6 ♣ — and partner responded 2♣, your rebid would be 2♡, up-the-line, not 2♠. By treating the reply to Stayman 2♣ in the same way, there is less likelihood of a moment of forgetfulness.

'Similar situations, similar approach' is a valuable technique for memorising system principles and various areas of bidding. Another area where this can be profitably applied is in seeking stoppers for no-trumps. Suppose you have the following hand:

♠ A K 2 ♡ 4 2 ◇ 8 3 2 ♣ A Q 9 7 4

What action would you take as South after each of these auctions?

(1)	WEST	NORTH	EAST	SOUTH
		1 ♡	No bid	2 ♣
	No bid	2 ♠	No bid	?

(2)	WEST	NORTH	EAST	SOUTH
		1 ♡	No bid	2 ♣
	2 ◇	No bid	No bid	?

(3)	WEST	NORTH	EAST	SOUTH
		1 ♡	No bid	2 ♣
	No bid	3 ♣	No bid	?

General consensus on the above situations would be 3◇ on (1) as fourth-suit-forcing, *asking* for a stopper for no-trumps, 3◇ on (2) as a cue-bid of the enemy suit, primarily *asking* for a stopper for no-trumps, and 3♠ on (3), *showing* a stopper in spades and *asking* for a stopper in diamonds for no-trumps.

Now, would it not make more sense to treat each of these situations in the same way so that in each case where stoppers are involved, bidding the critical suit is *asking* for the stopper? If you can convince your partners to ask for stoppers rather than show them, you will have fewer memory problems in this area of bidding. Asking for stoppers has a further practical advantage. If an opponent makes a lead-directing double, this is less effective if they double a stopper-asking bid than if they double a stopper-showing. example, suppose the auction has proceeded—

WEST	NORTH	EAST	SOUTH
1 ♠	No bid	2 ♣	No bid
3 ♣	No bid	3 ♡	Double
3NT	No bid	No bid	No bid

If 3♡ showed a stopper, the lead through that stopper could be dangerous. However, if 3♡ was asking for a stopper and 3NT showed that hearts were held, the lead coming up to that stopper would be far less advantageous to the defence.

The standard approach for stopper-showing or stopper-asking in auctions such as the above follows the up-the-line approach. Just as we bid four-card suits up-the-line, so that bypassing a suit denies four cards in that suit, so stoppers are shown up the line with a similar corollary when a suit is bypassed. Again, the same approach is used when cue bidding to a slam in standard methods. Controls are cue bid up-the-line and bypassing a suit other than trumps denies control in that suit. When the same principle is harnessed for several different areas, the degree of confusion is minimised as are the problems of recall.

Cue bidding is an area where the average player habitually has problems. Slam bidding is the least effective area for most partnerships and it is only because slams occur relatively rarely that partnerships can still do well despite this glaring ineffectuality. The 'play-it-again-and-again-Sam' principle can be utilised to assist partnerships wishing to improve their cue bidding to slams. One of the most effective practice methods works like this:

Just you and your partner engage in a practice session where you separate the court cards (A/K/Q/J) from the other cards, thus producing a deck of sixteen court cards and thirty-six others. The pack of thirty-six is shuffled and twenty cards are put aside face down. The remaining sixteen are shuffled together with the sixteen court cards, making a pack of thirty-two from which each player is dealt thirteen cards, the remaining six cards being left face down. The players preferably write down their auction and before comparing hands, each player should write down what holdings are expected in partner's hand. With this short deck, the hands are so powerful that game, small slam or grand slam is always the problem and by writing down the auction and the expected holdings, the partnership can discuss what should take place when significant differences of view arise. By dealing out thirty of such hands in a session, the partnership is telescoping three months slam experience into a short time, and as the situations come up again and again and the cue bidding sequences recur regularly, the partnership gains in confidence and the techniques of cue bidding are quickly mastered and remembered.

Another area where a partnership might do well to synchronise methods to alleviate the memory burden is actions over opposition opening bids. A double of 1 ♡ is played for takeout. What about a double of 2♡? Or 3♡? Or 4♡? Most partnerships use the same method over a weak two opening as over a one opening, double for takeout. A majority also use a double of three-openings for takeout and some extend this to the double of a 4♡ opening as well. The more areas that apply the same approach, the less that has to be remembered.

It is likewise sensible to play other takeout doubles to the same level as takeout doubles of opening bids. For example, if doubles of opening bids are for takeout only to the two-level, then it would be sensible to play negative doubles only to the two-level and responsive doubles to the same level as well. Partnerships who play responsive doubles to the two-level, negative doubles to the three-level and takeout doubles to the four-level are creating an unnecessary burden.

A similar consideration applies in a situation like this—

WEST	NORTH	EAST	SOUTH
1 ♡	1NT	No bid	2 ♣ . . .

Is that 2♣ bid natural or is it Stayman in your methods? There are sound arguments to play it either way, but a strong argument to have it as Stayman is to ease the memory strain. Many partnerships, including my favourite ones, play precisely the same methods over a 1NT overcall as over a 1NT opening, even when the range of these no-trump bids may be quite different. Thus, in one fell swoop, an extra area of learning and memorisation can be eliminated.

Learning New Conventions

There is a simple but effective way to learn almost any new convention. Take for example Extended Stayman, a method that is popular among partnerships who use a 4-point range for their 1NT opening. Suppose you and partner had agreed to play a 15-18 1NT and partner could not exist unless you agreed to play this version of Extended Stayman—

After 1NT : 2♣ opener will rebid as follows:

    2♦ = Both majors, 15–16 points
    2♡ = Hearts, denies four spades, 15–16 points
    2♠ = Spades, denies four hearts, 15–16 points
    2NT = Neither major, 15–16 points
    3♣ = Neither major, 17–18 points
    3♦ = Both majors, 1ᵀ–18 points
    3♡ = Hearts, denies four spades, 17–18 points
    3♠ = Spades, denies four hearts, 17–18 points

Now, without looking back to the text above can you recall what the sequence 1NT : 2♣, 3♦ showed? In the form above, there is a lot of information given and the learning process is made more difficult by the unwieldy material. To learn that by rote requires considerable effort. The simpler way is to summarise the convention and once the summary is learnt, the player is able to work out the correct bid or the meaning of partner's answer by applying the summary. The most effective summary of the above Extended Stayman is 'Two level is minimum, diamonds always show both majors'. Why was the diamond suit chosen to show both majors? To take advantage of the 'close-encounters' principle. 'Diamonds are a girl's best friend . . . diamonds are good news . . . both majors in reply to Stayman is good news . . . diamonds show both majors.'

In the Precision sequences 1♣ : 1♡, 2♡ and 1♣ : 1♠, 2♠, opener's second bid asks about the quality of the suit shown by responder who rebids as follows—

    Step 1 = No top honour in the suit (top honour = A, K or Q)
    Step 2 = One top honour in a five-card suit
    Step 3 = Two top honours in a five-card suit
    Step 4 = One top honour in a six-card or longer suit
    Step 5 = Two top honours in a six-card or longer suit
    Step 6 = All three top honours

Obviously it is much easier to remember the capsule summary of the above '0–1–2, 1–2–3'. It is a simple matter at the table to deduce the distinction between the two 1–2s.

Learning Judgment

The acquisition of judgment is the most difficult part of bridge and it usually takes years of regular play before a degree of judgment is developed. But it is possible to formulate simple principles and guidelines which will enable players to arrive at the correct decision most of the time. One of the most common is The Rule Of Three and Two for pre-emptive bids, i.e. that the playing tricks in a hand should be within three tricks of the bid made not vulnerable and within two tricks of the bid made vulnerable.

A lesser known guide is the 'True Romance Principle' which applies to hands such as

♠ A K Q J 6
♥ A K Q 4 3
♦ A
♣ Q 7

Suppose you open 2♣, game-force, and partner responds 2♦, negative. How would you continue? This is where the principle will help:

A good bridge hand is like a good romance—don't rush it.

A common mistake by the average player is to leap to 4♠ over the 2♦ reply, rushing it when it should be taken slowly and delicately. It is possible, although unlikely, that 4♠ could fail, but more importantly, 4♥ could be a better contract and even a slam is not out of the question (say partner held : ♠ 3   ♥ 9 8 7 5 2   ♦ 8 7 6 5   ♣ A 5 4, where partner would almost certainly pass 4♠ with 7♥ a fantastic spot). You should content yourself with 2♠ and explore partner's shape and strength as much as possible.

Another problem area for the intermediate player is when to use Stayman and when to stick with no-trumps. Suppose your partner has opened 1NT (12–14 points) and you hold—

♠ A J 5 3
♥ Q J 3
♦ K 9 8
♣ A 7 6

Would you bid 3NT direct or would you use Stayman 2♣ to try for the spade fit?

The answer to this sort of problem is not an easy one and either action can work some of the time. Experience indicates that the better prospect is to bid a direct 3NT. If a spade fit is not located, the information imparted to the opposition may assist them in the opening lead and their later defence. Even when a spade fit is located, the spade contract can be vastly inferior. For example, if the hands happened to be—

♠ K Q 6 4	opposite	♠ A J 5 3
♡ A 8 2		♡ Q J 3
◇ A 7 5		◇ K 9 8
♣ 9 5 3		♣ A 7 6

4♠ has very little genuine chance of success, while 3NT is laydown on anything but a club lead and no worse than 50% if a club is led. Even if opener's shape is 4–3–3–2 and not 4–3–3–3, there is no guarantee that 4♠ is better. For instance,

♠ K Q 6 4	opposite	♠ A J 5 3
♡ 7 4 2		♡ Q J 3
◇ A Q		◇ K 9 8
♣ K 8 5 4		♣ A 7 6

3NT is laydown while 4♠ might fail (if hearts are led and the third round is ruffed, for example) and even at pairs there are sufficient prospects for a tenth trick at no-trumps to make that spot preferable.

All of this experience and thinking is distilled in the maxim 'no shortage, no Stayman'. It will stand players in good stead until they have reached that stage of their bridge careers when resorting to maxims is no longer necessary.

For similar purposes, it is easier for many players to refer to an equation or a rule and easier for them to memorise that than to judge the correct action time and time again. After they have been through a given area often enough, they are then able to abandon the principles they used previously and proceed on the expertise and judgement they have acquired. One area that leans heavily on judgement is when to overcall and when to pass. Suppose you are second-in-hand and have to judge what to do after a 1♡ opening when you hold these cards—

♠ A Q
♡ 7 6 3
◇ A Q 2
♣ Q 7 5 3 2

Do you overcall 2♣, do you double or do you pass? You certainly have the high card values for action but your hand pattern is unsuitable for a double because of the lack of spade length. Many players would take action, wrongly, because of the power of the hand. To overcome the desire to take actions such as 2♣ on this kind of hand, a good test to apply is the SUIT QUALITY TEST. Given that the hand is strong enough to warrant an overcall, this test measures whether the suit is good enough for an overcall. Whereas opening bids are based on

[35]

high card strength, overcalls are based primarily on the length and strength of the suit, which is measured by the equation:

Length in suit to be overcalled + honours in suit to be overcalled should equal the number of tricks for which you are bidding.

Thus for a 1-level overcall, length + honours should be 7 or more, the suit for a 2-level overcall should measure 8 or more and so on. The A, K and Q count as full honour values but the jack and ten should be counted as honours only if the suit contains also at least one top honour. Applying this test to the hand above, the club suit measures only 6 (5 for length, 1 for honours), well below the 8 needed for a 2-level overcall. By contrast this hand

♠ 7 6
♥ 6 5
♦ Q 10 3
♣ A K 9 8 7 6

although weaker in high card strength is worth an overcall of 2♣, only just on the score of high card strength, but clearly on the score of the suit quality test.

The suit quality test can also be profitably applied in other areas where suit quality is a consideration, such as pre-emptive openings of three or four and for weak two openings (which should be no weaker than Q-10-x-x-x-x in order to satisfy the test). Once a player has had sufficient exposure and experience in this area, the suit quality test can be quietly discarded. Until then, it is a simple guide, easy to remember and adequately effective.

A similar approach can make players sufficiently expert in the area of low level penalty doubles. Suppose partner has opened with a suit bid and next player overcalls 1 ♠ or 2 ♦. Under what circumstances should you consider a penalty double? What trump strength is needed?

The conditions for a successful low level penalty double are a misfit with partner's suit and a combined total of at least half the high card strength plus a strong holding in their trump suit. What constitutes a satisfactory holding in their trump suit can be gauged by the Rule of 6 and 4:

Level at which they bid + Number of trumps in your hand = 6

Level at which they bid + Number of trump winners you hold = 4

For example, to double a 1 ♠ overcall you would need at least five trumps and three trump winners. To double a two-level overcall, four trumps including two trump winners are necessary.

Again, it is easier to remember the Rule of 6 and 4 than to try to cope with all the possible situations and again, once sufficient expertise has been acquired, the Rule of 6 and 4 can be conveniently forgotten. It has served its purpose.

(B) MEMORY METHODS FOR PROBLEMS IN THE PLAY

The following hand was played exactly as described. It is typical of the hands played every day in thousands of homes and hundreds of bridge clubs.

Dealer North
Both sides vulnerable

♠ A Q 6 3
♡ A 4 2
◇ A 10 9 2
♣ 7 4

♠ 9 8 4
♡ J 8 6 5
◇ 8 6
♣ A 10 8 2

```
      N
  W       E
      S
```

♠ K 7 2
♡ 10 7
◇ 7 5 4
♣ K J 9 5 3

♠ J 10 5
♡ K Q 9 3
◇ K Q J 3
♣ Q 6

WEST	NORTH	EAST	SOUTH
	1 ◇	No bid	1 ♡
No bid	1 ♠	No bid	3 ◇*
No bid	3 ♡	No bid	4 ♡†
No bid	No bid	No bid	

*Forcing in the North-South methods
†3♠ would have led to the superior 4♠ contract, but 4♡ was not foolish (certainly better than the doomed 3NT). When 3NT is known to be a poor bet and a 4-3 fit is to be chosen, holding the jack in the proposed trump suit is a definite advantage.

West led the ♣A and when East discouraged, the switch to a spade came. South ducked and East won the ♠K and the ♣K before exiting with a spade, taken by the jack. The contract now hinged on a favourable break in hearts, which you can see was not forthcoming. Declarer continued with a heart to the ace, a heart to the king, the ♡Q and, shrugging his shoulders, unsure whether the 9 of hearts was high or not, he led the ♡9. Thus instead of going one off, South went four down for no good reason.

Miscounting trumps is a common failing and not being certain whether a particular spot card is the high card or not is just as common. There are efficient methods for knowing when all the opposition trumps have been drawn and likewise one can train oneself to remember and be certain whether a particular card is high or not.

On most hands, the number of cards missing in a suit is important only for one or two suits, the trump suit and your long suit outside trumps. Many players count trumps or the cards in a long suit by chanting to themselves, 'Four have gone, and three have gone, and I trumped in once, and dummy has one left and I have three left, now let me see . . . how many have gone.' If they make no mistake in all these additions, they can come up with the right answer by deducting from thirteen. While this is not a difficult task, there are many ways in which it can go wrong. There are four or more additions plus one subtraction and a popular error is to forget that you or dummy or an opponent has trumped in.

The far more efficient method is to start the moment dummy appears and tell yourself how many cards there are in dummy and your own hand in the critical suit(s) and immediately tell yourself *how many cards they started with in the suit(s)*.

From then on, you need concern yourself only with the cards which they play in that suit. Thus, if you tell yourself at the outset that they began with five trumps, it will make no difference if you or dummy trumps in. They will still have started with five trumps. When it comes to drawing trumps, instead of the lengthy 'four have gone and three have gone . . .' routine, you are concerned only with the trumps which the opponents have played. The numbers with which you will be working are much smaller, the number of arithmetical steps far fewer and the chance of error is accordingly greatly reduced.

For example, if you and dummy hold eight trumps and the opponents five, your thoughts would go along these lines, '*They* started with five . . . we've played one round and they each played a trump . . . *they* are down to three . . . *they* both followed to the second round of trumps . . . good, there is only one trump missing' or perhaps '*They* started with five . . . we've played one round and *they* each played a trump . . . there are three missing . . . hullo, West showed out on the second round so *they* only produced one trump on that round . . . *they* are down to two trumps which are both with East . . .' You get the idea.

How to remember which of your cards are high
This problem is again best tackled at the beginning of a hand. Decide which of the cards held by the opponents are critical cards in your important suits

. . . which of their cards could conceivably become winners. From then on you need to watch out for only those critical cards. Here is a simple example but one which a novice has been known to get wrong more than once:

Dummy: K Q 4 3
Declarer: J 10 6 5

Declarer leads the jack, taken by the ace. Later in the play the king and queen are cashed and declarer is suddenly unsure whether the ten is a winner or not. The fact that the jack was played a lot earlier has been forgotten.

To overcome this, declarer should have said at the outset: 'The opponents have only *one* card in this suit that matters, the ace.' Once the ace was played, it should then and there register that all your top cards in this suit are winners because you took the trouble to work out that they had only one significant card.

Even if you think that example was trivial, hand after hand the question of *which are their critical cards* presents itself. If you do not address yourself to this question at the outset, you will make life tougher for yourself than it need be. Here are several other instances of working out which of their cards are critical:

(1) Dummy: J 6 2   (2) Dummy: J 6 2
      You: A K 3   You: A K 5 3

      (3) Dummy: J 6 2
           You: A K 9 3

(1) Only the queen is relevant. When you play the ace and king, you need to watch only for the queen.

(2) Only the queen is relevant in the high cards; the 3–3 division is relevant for the chance of an extra trick via the thirteenth.

(3) Now the queen and ten are both critical cards, as well as the 3–3 break.

(4) A K 10 5   (5) A K 9 5   (6) A K 8 5
      Q 3   Q 3   Q 3

(4) The critical card is the jack. If you play the queen, king and ace, you need watch only for the jack.

(5) This time the jack and ten are both key cards. When you play the queen, king and ace you must watch to see whether both the jack and ten fall. If so, the 9 is high; if not, the 9 will not be high.

(6) Here the jack, ten and nine are all vital. When you play the queen, king and ace, you need to see all three key cards appear for your eight to be a winner. Incidentally, if you play the queen and neither opponent drops the 9, 10 or J on the first round, the 8 will not become high.

(7)	7 6 5 4	(8)	Q J 5	(9)	A 4 2
	K Q 9 2		A 10 7 2		K Q 9 3

(7) The critical cards are the ace and the jack and ten. If the jack and ten drop on the first two rounds and you have drawn the ace, the 9 will be high.
(8) Initially, the critical card is the king and the 3–3 division is important. Suppose you lead the queen, low, low, 8 from West. Since you have the 7, the fall of the 8 now makes the 9 a critical card. Suppose, for example, you continue with the jack, East covers with the king, you win the ace and West follows with the 9. It is now vital that you noticed the fall of the 8 on the previous round, else you may miss that the 10 *and* the 7 are both winners.
(9) This is the combination from the complete hand on page 37. Critical are the jack and the ten.

What to do if you have lost count in trumps or another critical suit
Don't panic. Firstly, try to reconstruct the suit as it was at the beginning of the hand. How many cards in the suit did dummy have? How many did you hold? Then calculate how many cards the opponents held in that suit and go through how many rounds have been played. You may be able to tell how many cards are still missing.

If you are still unsure and the problem is in the trump suit, decide whether you can afford to play another round of trumps to check whether there might still be a trump (the lurker) in one of the opponent's hand. On many hands, you can comfortably afford an extra round of trumps and if so, you may as well use it to check out the position.

If you cannot afford another round of trumps, take a careful look at the cards played by the opposition on the previous round of trumps. If you played the queen and an opponent dropped the jack, there is a good chance that this was the last trump held by that opponent. The weaker the opposition the more likely it will be that this assumption is accurate. Novice players hate to part with their highish cards, even if they cannot possibly win a trick with them, so that the appearance of a significantly high card would imply that they hold no lower cards in the suit.

Against strong opposition, however, you cannot make the same inference with confidence. A good player would not think twice of following with the 4, 10 and jack from a holding such as J–10–9–4, leaving you to remember/guess/worry whether the 9 has gone or is still at large. Similarly, from 10–9–8 the expert might follow with the 9, then the 10. This kind of carding is part-and-parcel of the expert's technique in playing on the memory weaknesses of the novice player. It follows that when you are up against a top pair, you must redouble your concentration and your efforts in assessing how many cards are missing in the critical suits, which are the vital cards in those suits and so on.

Other critical cards

The opening lead. The actual card led and the choice of suits should be noted at once for future reference. They are usually a tell-tale sign, both for declarer and for the defence. If the opening lead is the 2, then that would be from at most a 4-card suit if the opponents are using fourth-highest leads. If they are using 3rd-or-5th-highest, the lead of the lowest possible card would be from either a 3-card or a 5-card suit. Against a no-trumps contract, it is almost always from a 5-card suit. If the lead is the 3 of a suit, the critical card is the 2. If it is visible then there are at most four cards in the suit with the leader. If it is not visible, the leader could have it and may hold a 5-card suit, if they are using fourth-highest. If they are playing 3rds-or-5ths, the sighting of the 2 indicates that the leader has three or five cards in the suit. If the 2 is not visible and the leader later plays it, the leader began with four cards in the suit (or six).

When you are in third seat, note carefully the card partner has led. Sometimes you can tell its significance at once. If partner has led the highest outstanding card, you should play partner to have a doubleton (or singleton) in the suit. If partner has led the lowest possible card, you should play partner to hold an honour card (or a singleton) in the suit, if your side is using M.U.D. This will frequently allow you to plan your defence at the outset. If you do not note the lead, however, you will be reduced to a guess what to do next. For example,

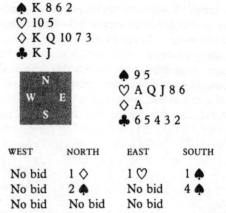

♠ K 8 6 2
♡ 10 5
◇ K Q 10 7 3
♣ K J

♠ 9 5
♡ A Q J 8 6
◇ A
♣ 6 5 4 3 2

The bidding has been:

WEST	NORTH	EAST	SOUTH
No bid	1 ◇	1 ♡	1 ♠
No bid	2 ♣	No bid	4 ♠
No bid	No bid	No bid	

West leads a heart. How do you defend?

If your immediate reaction is to ask which heart partner led, you are on the right track. The actual card chosen can be the deciding factor. Suppose partner's heart is (a) the two, (b) the nine, or (c) the four. How would you defend? In (a) partner has led lowest card, consistent only with a singleton or with an honour card if the partnership plays MUD (Middle-Up-Down from 3 or 4 cards without an honour card). The defence then should be: Win ♡ A, cash ◇ A, return ♡ 8 to partner's presumed king and partner returns a diamond for you to ruff. If the lead happened to be a singleton (unlikely, since that would give South five hearts), the defence still works as partner ruffs the second heart and returns a diamond.

In (b) partner has led the highest card, almost certainly a doubleton, and now the best chance is: Win ♡ A, cash ◇ A, lead a club to partner's ace and receive the diamond ruff. However, what if partner's ♡ 9 was really a singleton and partner does not have the ♣ A? This defence would fail.

A top partnership could solve that problem: when the ◇ A is cashed, West should read that as a singleton (why would East cash the ◇ A staring at those top diamonds in dummy?) and West should therefore give a suit-preference signal in diamonds to indicate the entry held—high diamond for the high suit, hearts, if the ♡ 9 was a singleton; lowest diamond for the low suit, clubs, if the ♡ 9 was not a singleton and the ♣ A is held.

In (c) the ♡ 4 lead is wholly ambiguous: it could be a singleto, doubleton from 4–3 or 4–2, a tripleton from 9–4–2, 9–4–3, 7–4–2, 7–4–3, from the king, such as K–9–4, K–7–4, K–9–7–4. After winning the ♡ A, East cashes the ◇ A and here the suit preference signal in diamonds as explained above would be the only sure way for East to determine whether to continue with a heart or a club at trick 3.

Making a note of the opening lead is also vital for declarer. A common example in quiz books is the opening lead of the 2 against a 1NT : 3NT auction. The leader later turns out to hold a singleton in another suit. Given that the lead of the 2 would be from at most four cards in the suit, declarer should deduce that the shape of the leader's hand is 4–4–4–1 since a 5-card suit would have been chosen as first preference.

The choice of suit for the opening lead also tells a tale. A trump lead tends to herald a favourable trump break. Leading from an ace-high suit in a trump contract such as A-x-x-x-x suggests that the leader has no safe lead to make, assuming the players are not novices. What would you do as West in this layout:

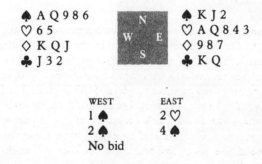

```
      ♠ A Q 9 8 6         N          ♠ K J 2
      ♡ 6 5          W         E      ♡ A Q 8 4 3
      ◇ K Q J             S          ◇ 9 8 7
      ♣ J 3 2                         ♣ K Q
```

WEST	EAST
1 ♠	2 ♡
2 ♠	4 ♠
No bid	

The opening lead is the ♡ 2. How should you plan the play?

You should note at once the fact that your opponent has led a suit bid by dummy. It would be naïve to take a finesse at trick one in such circumstances. A competent opponent would not be leading hearts on this auction without a good reason. If you finesse, you find very quickly that South wins the king and returns a heart for partner to ruff and two aces later, you are one off. When they lead a side suit that you or dummy have bid, most of the time it will be a singleton lead.

The critical round of a suit is the second round. While on some occasions you can tell what is happening on the first round, most of the time you will have to wait until the second round to be sure of the position. By noting carefully what takes place on the second round you will have a clearer idea what to do. Suppose you are defending as East in this situation:

    (Dummy)   ♠ Q 3
                    ♡ Q 7 6
                    ◇ A K 10 8 6
                    ♣ 7 6 3

                            ♠ 4   (You)
                            ♡ A K J 10 2
                            ◇ Q J 3
                            ♣ J 5 4 2

With both sides vulnerable, East opens 1♡ and South's jump to 4♠ ends the bidding. West leads the ♡ 5. How should East plan the play?

Since you cannot tell partner's holding from the lead of the 5, you must play a second round of hearts after winning the first trick. How would you continue if West played the ♡ 4 at trick 2? What if West's second heart were the 9?

By checking out the suit after the second round has been played, you can see that in the first case, West has shown a doubleton and the missing heart is with declarer. You therefore cash a third heart before leading a club, defeating South who has ♠ A K 10 9 8 7 5 2 ♡ 9 8 3 ◇ 5 ♣ K. In the second situation, West's play of ♡ 5 followed by ♡ 9 indicates that West has the thirteenth heart. It would therefore be foolish to play a third heart and a club switch is indicated, again beating South who has ♠ A K 10 9 8 7 5 2 ♡ 8 3 ◇ 5 ♣ K 8.

Note that if you switch to clubs at trick 3 in the first case, declarer will succeed, by discarding the heart loser on the second diamond winner later, while if you continue with a third heart in the second situation, declarer can in fact make eleven tricks, by setting up the diamonds for two club discards. *Critical tricks to be noted are those where a player shows out of a suit or where something startling occurs.* By paying special attention at those moments you will be better placed to recall the important information later in the hand. When a player shows out of a suit, make a mental note of the number of cards with which that player started and how the suit was originally divided around the table. Sometimes the fall of a key card can be critical. Suppose you are playing in a pairs event as West on the following layout:

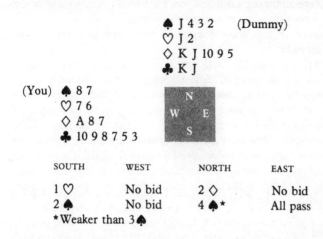

```
                    ♠ J 4 3 2      (Dummy)
                    ♡ J 2
                    ◊ K J 10 9 5
                    ♣ K J
(You)   ♠ 8 7
        ♡ 7 6                      N
        ◊ A 8 7               W         E
        ♣ 10 9 8 7 5 3            S
```

SOUTH	WEST	NORTH	EAST
1 ♡	No bid	2 ◊	No bid
2 ♠	No bid	4 ♠ ★	All pass
★Weaker than 3♠			

You lead the ♣ 10 and partner wins dummy's jack with the queen. Partner's ♣ A is ruffed by declarer, who cashes the ♠ A and K, partner following with the 9 and Q. Declarer now leads the ◊ 4. Do you play low and hope declarer misguesses or do you rise with the ◊ A?

The startling play so far has been partner's ♠ Q falling on the second round. This marks South with five spades and therefore six hearts because of the 1 ♡ opening (with 5-5, the opening would have been 1♠). Therefore South can have only one diamond and if you do not grab your ace of diamonds now, you will never take it, since South has no guess in diamonds with an original holding of   ♠ A K 10 6 5   ♡ A Q 10 9 5 4   ◊ 4   ♣ 3.

It is clear from this example that you must force yourself to pay close attention to the cards played and just as close attention to the bidding. If you have forgotten the bidding when the play begins, you are operating under a severe handicap. If you are not involved in the bidding, do not take this time off to relax (you can relax when you are dummy) but make a concerted effort to understand the auction and the high card values and the shape which declarer and dummy have revealed. Time so spent is well worth the effort. Part of this discipline is to ensure that you actually look at each card played. Do not be hesitant about taking a second look. At duplicate do not turn your own card over until you have satisfied yourself that you have seen the cards played. If written bidding or bidding boxes are used, again make sure that you deliberately look at each bid made. Even at the top level, there are many instances of players missing a bid.

How to recover if you have forgotten the card partner led or partner's signal

If you find that you have failed to notice the actual card partner played on the first round of a suit or the first part of partner's signal, do not panic. You may be able to recover by watching carefully the second card partner plays in that particular suit or the second part of partner's signal. If on the next round of the suit, partner plays the lowest possible card, you can deduce that partner has played high-low. Likewise, if the second part of a signal from partner is the lowest possible card, partner has given a high-low signal. On the other hand, if partner's second card is an unusually high card, one that makes more impression than partner's first card obviously did, assume partner to have played low-high and take it from there.

On signalling

The 'freak-out' principle is at work in using high-card-encouraging as the basis for standard signalling. A low card makes little impression. When partner sees you drop an 8 or a 9, that is intended to make a significant impression. Below expert level other signalling methods are less effective since the cards played do not have the same impact. Even though other signalling methods have definite theoretical advantages (such as reverse signals, i.e. lowest-card-encouraging) they should not be introduced for beginners or novice players. Only once a partnership has reached a good stage of competent defence, should consideration be given to adopting non-standard signals.

When you are using high-encouraging, you signal with the highest card you can afford. The higher the card, the greater the impact and the more effective is the operation of the 'freak-out' principle. Even at the very top level, players make use of this principle to ensure partner pays attention to their signals. In reporting on a deal from the France versus Italy match in the 1983 European Championships, Luigi Filippo d'Amico of Italy began his report this way: 'Playing with Arturo Franco, you'd better obey his orders or you will be in a rare spot. He once told his partner, Dano de Falco: "When I call for a spade, you are not supposed to think. You play a spade. If you haven't got a spade, you find one in another pack of cards and come back and lead it. Understand?" '

Remembering which card to keep and which to discard

A familiar principle in discarding is 'keep length with dummy'. In other words, if dummy has four cards or more in a suit and you also have four or more cards in that suit, you should retain your length if you can possibly win a trick. For example:

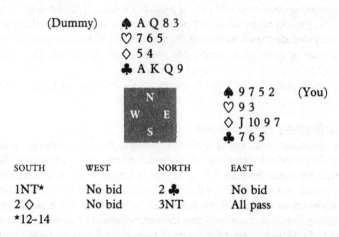

(Dummy)	♠ A Q 8 3
	♡ 7 6 5
	◇ 5 4
	♣ A K Q 9

♠ 9 7 5 2   (You)
♡ 9 3
◇ J 10 9 7
♣ 7 6 5

SOUTH	WEST	NORTH	EAST
1NT*	No bid	2♣	No bid
2◇	No bid	3NT	All pass
*12–14			

After a routine Stayman auction, partner leads the ♡ K, winning, and the ♡ Q continuation is taken by declarer's ace. South continues with the ♣ J and a club to dummy. All follow to the third round of clubs and when the fourth round is led from dummy, you have to make a discard. What do you let go?

At the table nine defenders out of ten would pitch a spade. The correct discard is a diamond, because you have to keep length with dummy's spades. Declarer holds: ♠ K 6 4   ♡ A 8   ◇ K Q 6 3 2   ♣ J 8 4. If East lets a spade go, declarer has four spade tricks for the game. If East retains the spades, declarer will end one short.

Precisely the same principle applies if declarer is known to have length in the suit: you must retain your length in that suit. The information about declarer's lengths will come from the bidding or from partner showing out in a suit or from partner's signalling. Another clue as to what to keep and what to let go arises in this kind of situation:

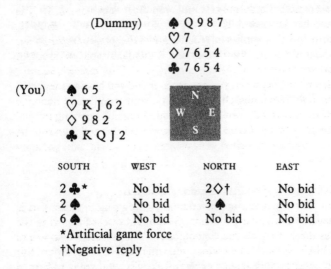

	(Dummy)	♠ Q 9 8 7
		♡ 7
		♢ 7 6 5 4
		♣ 7 6 5 4

(You) ♠ 6 5
♡ K J 6 2
♢ 9 8 2
♣ K Q J 2

SOUTH	WEST	NORTH	EAST
2 ♣ *	No bid	2 ♢ †	No bid
2 ♠	No bid	3 ♠	No bid
6 ♠	No bid	No bid	No bid

*Artificial game force
†Negative reply

Playing pairs, you lead the ♣ K taken by South's ace. Declarer plays two rounds of trumps on which East discards hearts. Declarer cashes the ♡ A and ruffs a heart in dummy, partner following. Declarer plays a trump to hand and plays off his other four trumps and the A–K of diamonds. This leaves one card remaining.

Do you hang on to your ♣Q or your ♡K?

Even without any helpful signalling or discarding from partner, this kind of problem is not hard to solve. If declarer's remaining card were a heart, it would have been ruffed in dummy. Hence, you must keep your ♣ Q. The complete South hand was ♠ A K J 10 4 3 2   ♡ A 9   ◇ A K   ♣ A 10.

Thus the principle that applies is: *If declarer had the option of ruffing a suit in dummy but did not do so, discard that suit.* A similar simple guide is *Has declarer already trumped one of the key suits in hand? If so, discard that suit.*

It follows from this that when you are declarer and you have an inevitable loser and your only remaining chance is to run your trumps and hope the defenders discard incorrectly, you should avoid, if possible, coming to hand by ruffing one of the suits. Better to play a trump to hand and then run the rest of the trumps or lead to one of your winners in an outside suit and then run your trumps.

How to cause your opponents memory problems

A well-known ploy when you are defending and you cannot follow suit is that if you have no particular problems, you should discard a card of the same colour as the suit which you cannot follow. The principle is known as 'Red on red; black on black'. Of course, you will not deceive an expert, but most of us do not play only against experts. Likewise, you are not likely to mislead a competent opponent early in the session. After 2–3 hours of a session, the concentration of most players starts to flag. That is when declarer may not notice that you played a diamond when hearts are trumps and may thus miscount trumps, thinking they have all been drawn when in fact a trump is still out.

Another tried manoeuvre is to discard a useless card in dummy's long suit. If declarer registers merely that you have not followed suit and fails to register the actual suit discarded, declarer may miscount the hand later. That explains what happened on this deal:

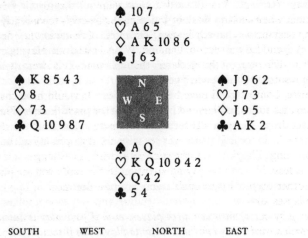

```
                    ♠ 10 7
                    ♡ A 6 5
                    ◇ A K 10 8 6
                    ♣ J 6 3
  ♠ K 8 5 4 3                        ♠ J 9 6 2
  ♡ 8                                ♡ J 7 3
  ◇ 7 3                              ◇ J 9 5
  ♣ Q 10 9 8 7                       ♣ A K 2
                    ♠ A Q
                    ♡ K Q 10 9 4 2
                    ◇ Q 4 2
                    ♣ 5 4
```

SOUTH	WEST	NORTH	EAST
1 ♡	No bid	2 ◇	No bid
2 ♡	No bid	4 ♡	All pass

West led the ♣ 10 and declarer ruffed the third round of clubs. The ♡ K, ♡ Q and a heart to the ace drew trumps. Then came the ◇ Q and a diamond to the king. Declarer abandoned diamonds and took the spade finesse, restricting the tally to ten tricks and a horrible board at pairs for North-South. Since eleven tricks are mama-papa, how could this come about?

West was a veteran campaigner and knew that South was not naïve enough to fall for red on red, so West discarded a spade on the second round of hearts to make sure that South knew West was out of trumps. Then on the third round of trumps, West discarded a low diamond, making a key discard at a moment when declarer was not watching the discards too intently since the trump position was already known. The effect of that was when declarer won the ◇ Q and led the second diamond, West showed out. Having missed the earlier diamond pitch, declarer thought diamonds were 4-1 and therefore resorted to the spade finesse.

Of course, South should have been more alert. It would have cost him nothing to cash the third diamond before trying the spade finesse. When the jack in fact drops, declarer's recovery is automatic. That does not detract from West's little ploy. If you never set traps for the opposition, they will never go wrong. The time to make such a discard in a key long suit is when declarer is least likely to be paying attention to the cards you are playing.

Some other useful tips to enable you to make the most of opponents' memory lapses are:

(1) Never play out of turn as fourth player, even if your play is automatic. Never detach a card from your hand ready to play, even if that play is forced.

Declarer may have led a card which is high but declarer may not remember that it is high. It may be the last card in the suit, but declarer may have forgotten that and may be intending to trump it. If fourth player discards before declarer has played, declarer's dilemma may be solved. Likewise, declarer may think a card is high when in fact it is not, or declarer may think it is the thirteenth when actually you hold a higher card. If you reveal your card too soon, declarer may avoid a foolish mistake.

Here is an example of how an inexperienced declarer saved a defender from an awkward guess at the end of the play:

Dealer North
Both vulnerable

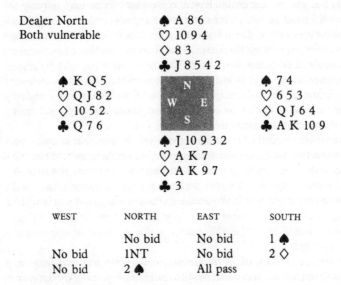

♠ A 8 6
♡ 10 9 4
◇ 8 3
♣ J 8 5 4 2

♠ K Q 5
♡ Q J 8 2
◇ 10 5 2
♣ Q 7 6

♠ 7 4
♡ 6 5 3
◇ Q J 6 4
♣ A K 10 9

♠ J 10 9 3 2
♡ A K 7
◇ A K 9 7
♣ 3

WEST	NORTH	EAST	SOUTH
	No bid	No bid	1 ♠
No bid	1NT	No bid	2 ◇
No bid	2 ♠	All pass	

In practice the play went as follows:

West led the queen of hearts, taken by the ace. The ace and king of diamonds were cashed and a third diamond was ruffed in dummy. Declarer came back to the king of hearts and instead of leading the fourth diamond to ruff in dummy, declarer led a low spade and when West played low, the ♠ 8 was finessed successfully. The ♠ A was cashed and declarer led a club from dummy. East rose with the king and played a third round of hearts, won by West's jack. West cashed the ♠ K and instead of playing the ♣ Q, West exited with the thirteenth heart at trick eleven, ruffed by South. South had the ♠ J and ◇ 9 left and East was holding the ♣ A and ◇ Q. At trick twelve South led the ♠ J and East had to decide whether to hold the top club or the top diamond. Just as East was thinking about what to do, South faced the ◇ 9, conceding the last trick.

That was quite foolish of South for East might have discarded the wrong card. True, East should know that South has a diamond left if East was counting, but it is just as true that East may have made a mistake. Most of the defenders we meet do not count out every hand and even if the chance of East making the wrong discard is only 10%, it is still a better move than supinely conceding the trick to East. Moral: Do not save the opposition from a guess. Make them work for their tricks.

(2) As declarer, when you intend to run your trumps and hope the defenders make a discarding error, throw the relevant suit from dummy early and keep irrelevant cards in dummy to maximise your chances of memory lapse with a defender as to what has gone and what is still left.

Of course you will have to be a bit more subtle than that and mix your discarding tactics, since otherwise the opposition would know to throw what you keep in dummy and keep what you throw from dummy. Nevertheless, on the majority of occasions it will pay you to pitch early from dummy the suit you are keeping in hand. An excellent situation for this is a holding like:

Dummy: A 6 3 2
Declarer: K 5 4

If you retain the four cards in dummy, most defenders will hang on to their length in that suit (keep length with dummy). If you can discard two of those cards from dummy, you will be amazed how often both defenders let the suit go, giving you a present of a third trick with the 5.

TIPS ON REMEMBERING CERTAIN PRINCIPLES OF PLAY

(1) On opening leads
(a) M.U.D. The mnemonic MUD for middle-up-down is a handy memory device for the lead of the second card from holdings of 3 or 4 cards without an honour card.
(b) When you hold 4 or more trumps, it is usually good strategy to lead your side's longest suit (often your own longest suit), to try to force declarer to trump in. If you can make declarer trump in often enough, declarer may lose

control of the hand. The principle that applies here is 'TRUMP LENGTH, LEAD LENGTH' and is well illustrated by this deal:

Dealer South
Both vulnerable

♠ A K
♡ J 8 7
◊ 7 6 5 2
♣ K J 10 9

♠ 7 6 2
♡ A K Q 2
◊ J 9 8 4 3
♣ 5

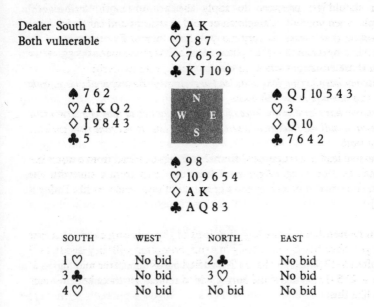

♠ Q J 10 5 4 3
♡ 3
◊ Q 10
♣ 7 6 4 2

♠ 9 8
♡ 10 9 6 5 4
◊ A K
♣ A Q 8 3

SOUTH	WEST	NORTH	EAST
1 ♡	No bid	2 ♣	No bid
3 ♣	No bid	3 ♡	No bid
4 ♡	No bid	No bid	No bid

4♡ is the best contract on the North-South cards, requiring no more than a 3–2 break in trumps to succeed. 3NT would be beaten on a spade or a diamond lead and 5♣ is clearly hopeless. Even with the 4–1 break, most declarers would succeed. Many Wests would lead the singleton club and some would lead trumps. Following the 'Trump-length, lead-length' principle, West should lead a diamond.

On anything but a diamond lead, declarer succeeds, simply by leading trumps at every opportunity and finally drawing West's ♡2. On a diamond lead, although South is very well-heeled in diamonds indeed, West's tactics will win the day. South wins the diamond and leads a trump. West wins and leads a diamond. South wins and leads a second trump. West wins and leads a third diamond, forcing South to ruff. South now has ♡10–9 and West has ♡A–2. If South leads a third round of trumps, the contract will go two down as West wins and forces out South's last trump and still holds the ♡2 as the last trump together with a diamond winner. The best that South can do is abandon trumps and allow West to ruff with the ♡ 2 on the clubs.

You should be prepared to apply the 'trump-length, lead-length' principle when you hold a singleton or void in trumps and can judge from the bidding that partner is very likely to hold four or five trumps.

(c) In deciding when to make a passive lead and when to make an aggressive lead in those situations when no clearcut lead presents itself:

If dummy has shown a long suit, lead aggressively. Be prepared to lead from one or two honours in an unbid suit.

If dummy has given no evidence of a long, strong suit so that you do not fear that declarer will easily discard losers, go passive and do not take risks with the opening lead.

A passive lead is a trump lead from 2 or 3 rags or a lead from a worthless suit such as 3 or 4 rags. Aggressive leads are leads from a suit with one honour such as K-x-x-x or Q-x-x-x or a suit with two honours like K-J-x-x or Q-J-x-x.

(2) On remembering the key divisions of the missing cards in a suit

When you have five cards missing in a suit, how often will they divide 3–2? How often 4–1? When you have a 7-card fit, how often will the missing cards divide 4–2? 5–1? A simple memory guide to remember these key divisions works like this:

For these four main breaks, simply turn the figures back to front. Thus—

The 3–2 break occurs $\frac{2}{3}$ of the time.
The 4–1 break occurs $\frac{1}{4}$ of the time.
The 4–2 break occurs $\frac{2}{4}$ or 50% of the time
and the 5–1 break about 20% of the time.

While not absolutely accurate, these are correct within a few percent and are certainly close enough for all practical considerations at the table. Equally this does not work for all divisions (the 3–3 break does not occur 100% of the time!) and for most of the other breaks the figures are too far from reality to be useful. Nevertheless, the 8-card combined holding with 5 cards missing and the 7-card combined holding with 6 cards missing are the situations that occur most frequently and this is a simple way to remember the figures for those cases.

Another handy guide is this area is the Even-Odd, Odd-Even rule:

If an EVEN number of cards is missing, the split will be ODD most of the time.

If an ODD number of cards is missing, the split will be EVEN most of the time.

Thus if 5 cards are missing, the even split 3–2 is better than 50–50. If 7 cards are missing, the even split 4–3 is better than 50–50, and so on. However, if the number of cards missing is 4, the 3–1 break (odd) is more likely than the 2–2 break (even) and if 6 cards are missing the 4–2 break (odd) is more probable than the even break of 3–3. Likewise, if 8 cards are missing, the 5–3 odd break is more common than the 4–4 even break. The only place where this excellent guide breaks down is when there are 2 cards missing, for here the even break 1–1 is marginally ahead of the odd 2–0 break (52% to 48%).

(3) On how to handle various card combinations

(a) 'Eight ever, nine never': This is intended to be a guide to playing the following combinations *provided that there are no other factors to be taken into account.*

	(i) Dummy:	K J 5 4		(ii) Dummy:	K J 5 4
	Declarer:	A 6 3 2		Declarer:	A 7 6 3 2

'Eight ever' means that with eight cards missing the queen, the correct play is 'always (ever) finesse'. In (i) you should cash the ace and then lead low, playing dummy's *jack* if West plays low. 'Nine never' means that if you have nine cards missing the queen, you should never finesse, so that in (ii) you cash the ace and then lead low, playing dummy's *king* if West plays low.

The trouble with guidelines like this is that average players treat them as universal truths instead of the mere guides which they are intended to be. Other similar guides which are treated with awe instead of with suspicion are 'Second hand low', 'Third Hand High', 'Cover An Honour With An Honour', 'Lead Through Strength, Lead Up To Weakness' . . . In all these cases there are usually other factors to be taken into account and to be reasonably functional, these guides have to be hedged with heavy qualification.

For example, here is a simple example of when it would be wrong to apply 'Eight ever, nine never'.

♠ K J 4   N   ♠ 6 5
♡ A 5   W   E   ♡ 7 4 3
◇ A J 6 4 3   S   ◇ K 7 5 2
♣ 10 6 5   ♣ A K Q J

West is playing Three No-Trumps. How would you plan the play if:

   (i) North leads the ♠ 3 and South plays the Q?
   (ii) North leads the ♡ 6 and South plays the Q?

In (i) you should win the ♠ K at trick one, play off four rounds of clubs if you wish, discarding a heart, but then play ◇ K and continue with a low diamond, playing the jack if South plays low. As long as South does not obtain the lead, West's J-4 of spades is safe from attack and the contract is assured. In (ii), however, after the ♡ A has been dislodged, you are in jeopardy if you let the opposition in and there is no 'safe' and no 'dangerous' opponent. Now you must play the diamonds to maximise your chances of not losing the lead at all, so that after taking your clubs, ◇ K and a diamond to the ace is your best line.

(b) Precautionary plays: How should you handle these combinations?

   (i) Dummy: K 10 6 5   (ii) Dummy: K 7 6 5
       Declarer: A Q 9 4 3   Declarer: A Q 9 4 3

The holdings look similar, yet the correct play differs. In (i), you should cash the ace or queen first, while in (ii) you should play the king on the first round. In (i), the correct play guards against either opponent holding four to the jack, since this would show up on the first round, allowing you to finesse against the jack later. In (ii), the correct play guards against East holding J-10-8-2, since this would show up and two finesses can then be taken against East. (If West has J-10-8-2, a loser is inevitable.)

The principles that cover these and similar situations are:
If missing the jack (one honour), keep one higher honour in each hand.
If missing jack and ten (two honours), keep two honours together in one hand.

Easing the Struggle

(c) Surround plays:

(i) NORTH (Dummy)
A 9 5

EAST (You)
Q 10 8 2

(ii) NORTH (Dummy)
10 6 4

EAST (You)
K J 9 5

The rule that covers positions like this is:

When you are leading up to dummy AND dummy has the jack, ten or nine, which you have 'surrounded' (the cards either side of dummy's jack, ten or nine), then if you have two cards higher than dummy's 'surrounded' card, imagine that dummy's 'surrounded' card is in your own hand and lead the card that you would lead if that were the case.

In (i), dummy has the 9 which you surround with your 10 and 8. You have two cards higher than the 9, so you imagine the 9 in your own hand, giving you Q–10–9–8–2 from which the standard lead would be the 10, top of the sequence. Accordingly, you should lead the 10 in the actual case. This caters for this layout:

A 9 5

K 6 3   Q 10 8 2

J 7 4

If East does lead the 10, declarer can come to only one trick. If East leads the 2 or 8, declarer can come to a second trick by playing low from hand. If East leads the queen, declarer can duck all round or win with the ace, but the defence cannot lead the suit again without giving declarer a second trick. If declarer has K–J–x, East's play is immaterial.

In (ii), dummy's 10 is surrounded by the J and 9 and East has two honours higher than the 10. Imagine the 10 in East's hand, giving East K–J–10–9–5 from which the jack is the standard lead. Hence, the jack should be led in the actual layout, catering for:

10 6 4   or   10 6 4

A 3 2 K J 9 5   7 3 2 K J 9 5

Q 8 7   A Q 8

In the first case, if East leads the jack, the defence can take all the tricks in the suit, but if East leads low, South comes to a trick by playing low from hand. In the second case, the lead of the jack holds declarer to two tricks (to which declarer is entitled with A–Q sitting over the king), but if East leads low, declarer can come to three tricks by playing low from hand, allowing dummy's 10 to win and following with a finesse of the queen.

(4) The Rule of Eleven and the Law of Fifteen

Most players are familiar with the Rule of Eleven which states that if the lead was the fourth-highest of a long suit, then the answer after deducting the card led from 11 tells you the number of cards higher than that card in the other three hands (outside the leader's hand). For example, if the 4 is led, $11 - 4 = 7$ so that there are seven cards higher than the 4 in the other three hands. A perusal of dummy's cards and your own cards indicates how many cards higher than the card led are in the remaining hand. The Rule of Eleven can be used by third hand (partner of the leader) or by declarer, who freqently can make better use of it than the defenders. For example,

Dummy: A 9 4
Declarer: Q J 5

If West leads the 7, declarer should play dummy's 9. If the lead is fourth-highest (from K–10–8–7), $11 - 7 = 4$, so that the other hands have four cards higher than the 7 and since declarer can see four cards higher than the 7 in dummy and in hand, East will be unable to beat the 7. By inserting dummy's 9, declarer will win the trick and can later take another finesse in the suit for three tricks in all. If declarer plays low from dummy, declarer cannot guarantee a third trick. If it turns out that East wins the king at trick one, it indicates that West's lead was not fourth-highest after all.

What should you do, however, if the opponents do not use fourth-highest but are leading 3rd-highest, or 5th-highest? How can you calculate their holdings then? The rule to apply is found by deducting their approach to leads from 15, so that if they lead *fourth*-highest, $15 - 4 = 11$, so that the Rule of Eleven is used. If they are using *third*-highest, $15 - 3 = 12$, so you apply the Rule of Twelve. If the lead is *fifth*-highest, $15 - 5 = 10$, so the Rule of Ten would be used. Easy, isn't it?

EXERCISES FOR SECTION TWO

1. After a weak two opening, many partnerships use the Ogust 2NT convention to discover the strength of opener's weak two and the quality of the suit opened. Assuming that the range of the weak two is 6–10 high card points and the test for suit quality is based on the question whether the suit is headed by one or by two of the top three honours (A, K or Q only), what simple formula could you produce to memorise the following—

The Ogust Convention:
    After 2♡ : 2NT or 2♠ : 2NT, opener rebids as follows—
        3♣ = 6–8 points, one of the top three honours
        3◇ = 6–8 points, two of the top three honours
        3♡ = 9–10 points, one of the top three honours
        3♠ = 9–10 points, two of the top three honours
        3NT = 9–10 points, all three top honours, A–K–Q–x–x–x or better

2. Suppose you and partner had agreed to play a variation to the Precision system in which a 2♠ reply to the 1♣ opening showed 8 or more points and a 4–4–4–1 shape, a problem area for that system, and suppose that you agreed that 2NT by the opener would ask for the singleton. How would you frame a rule to cover this approach?

After 1♣ : 2♠, 2NT responder shows the singleton as follows:
    3♣ = singleton spade
    3◇ = singleton heart
    3♡ = singleton diamond
    3♠ = singleton club

And what simple rule would cover this continuation?

After 1♣ : 2♠, 2NT responder shows the singleton as follows:
    3♣ = singleton diamond
    3◇ = singleton heart
    3♡ = singleton spade
    3♠ = singleton club

3. Suppose you hold:

> ♠ J 7 5 3 2
> ♡ A K Q
> ◇ A 2
> ♣ 7 6 5

You are South and the bidding has developed:

(a)

WEST	NORTH	EAST	SOUTH
1 ♡	No bid	2 ◇	?

Do you bid 2♠? If not, what action do you take?

(b)

WEST	NORTH	EAST	SOUTH
1 ♡	No bid	2 ♡	?

Do you bid 2♠? If not, what action do you take?

(c)

WEST	NORTH	EAST	SOUTH
	1 ♣	1 ♠	?

Assuming a double here would not be negative, should you double for penalties?

4.

♠ 7 6 5	N	♠ K 8
♡ Q 7	W E	♡ A K 10 3
◇ K Q 9 3 2	S	◇ A 6
♣ A J 6		♣ Q 10 9 8 3

West is playing in 3NT and receives the ♠ 3 lead. Dummy's king holds at trick one and South plays the 9.

(a) How do you think the spade suit is divided?
(b) Which cards are critical in hearts and diamonds?
(c) How you plan the play?

5.   (Dummy)   ♠ J 9 8 6
                         ♡ J 9 6
                         ◇ K 7
                         ♣ A K Q J

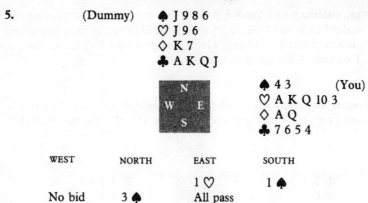

                                        ♠ 4 3   (You)
                                        ♡ A K Q 10 3
                                        ◇ A Q
                                        ♣ 7 6 5 4

WEST	NORTH	EAST	SOUTH
		1 ♡	1 ♠
No bid	3 ♠	All pass	

West leads the ♡ 5 and you win the first trick. You cash another top heart. How would you continue if West followed with (a) the 2? (b) the 8?

6.   (Dummy)   ♠ 9 7 6 5
                         ♡ A K 3 2
                         ◇ A 3
                         ♣ Q J 10

                                        ♠ 4   (You)
                                        ♡ Q 10 8 6
                                        ◇ Q J 4
                                        ♣ 7 5 4 3 2

The bidding, at pairs duplicate:

WEST	NORTH	EAST	SOUTH
No bid	1NT(1)	No bid	3 ♠
No bid	4 ◇ (2)	No bid	5 ♣ (2)
No bid	5 ♡ (2)	No bid	6 ♠
No bid	No bid	No bid	

(1) *12 – 14*
(2) *cue bids*

West leads the ♣ 9 and South wins the ace. South plays the ♠ A–K, West following. What do you discard?

South continues with the ♣ K and a club to the queen, West showing out on the third club, and then spades are continued, West not following to the third round of trumps. Dummy's last six cards are the four hearts and the two diamonds. What are your last six cards?

7. Your trump suit is A–K–3–2 opposite 8–7–5–4? What are the chances you will have only one trump loser? What are the odds the suit will break 4–1?

8.

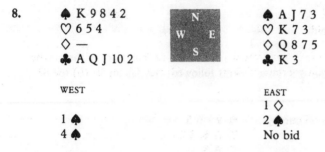

♠ K 9 8 4 2	♠ A J 7 3
♡ 6 5 4	♡ K 7 3
◇ —	◇ Q 8 7 5
♣ A Q J 10 2	♣ K 3

WEST	EAST
	1 ◇
1 ♠	2 ♠
4 ♠	No bid

West is playing 4♠. How would you plan the play if
(a) North leads the ◇ K, ruffed by West?
(b) North leads the ♡ Q and the defence take the first three tricks in hearts?

9. How do you handle these combinations to minimise the risk of losing a trick?

    (a)   Dummy: K Q 8 2
           Declarer: A 9 7 4 3

    (b)   Dummy: A Q 9 3
           Declarer: K 10 4 2

    (c)   Dummy: A K 9 2
           Declarer: Q 6 4 3

10.　　　　　　(Dummy)

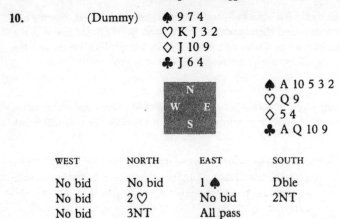

```
                  ♠ 9 7 4
                  ♡ K J 3 2
                  ◇ J 10 9
                  ♣ J 6 4
                              ♠ A 10 5 3 2
        N                     ♡ Q 9
     W     E                  ◇ 5 4
        S                     ♣ A Q 10 9
```

WEST	NORTH	EAST	SOUTH
No bid	No bid	1 ♠	Dble
No bid	2 ♡	No bid	2NT
No bid	3NT	All pass	

West leads the ♠ 8. How should East plan the defence?

(Answers to exercises are in Appendix II, page 89)

Section Three: Making It All Worthwhile

ADVANCED TO EXPERT TECHNIQUES

(A) MEMORY METHODS FOR THE BIDDING

As far as possible, one should minimise the strain on memory so that one's attention can be focussed on judgement in the bidding, or the opening lead or the later play or defence. There are two aspects to this:

(1) Make your system as easy to learn and memorise as possible.

(2) Once the system has been settled, learn it thoroughly until it requires almost no conscious effort to recognise the meaning of any bid or any sequence in the system.

(1) System construction

(a) Prefer to construct a system according to general principles rather than on random meanings, which may be theoretically efficient but which place a heavy emphasis on rote learning. It is easier to come to grips with a system where one can understand the underlying logic than one where most sequences have no common ground.

There is less chance of error if there is a general rule that can be applied to similar situations. This is making use of the 'close-encounters' principle. If in a situation of pressure in a critical match your memory does falter, then if the learning has been by rote, there is nothing to fall back on, but if one has a general rule, one can refer to that and deduce the correct meaning of partner's bid or the correct bid that one must make oneself. A slight loss of efficiency is acceptable if in consequence it makes the system more likely to be remembered. Obviously it is preferable to play a good system that will be remembered than an excellent system that might be forgotten.

For example, suppose that you and partner wished to use 4NT in slam-going auctions as a trump ask for the king and queen of trumps after a major suit has been set as trumps. Which of these two sets of replies would you choose?

    (i)   5 ♣ = queen of trumps
          5 ◇ = king of trumps
          5-agreed-major = neither king, nor queen
          5-other-major = both king and queen

    (ii) 5 ♣ = queen of trumps
          5 ◇ = king of trumps
          5 ♡ = neither king, nor queen
          5 ♠ = both king and queen

Scheme (ii) is the easier to remember since there is only one set of answers which stay the same no matter which suit is trumps and the scheme can be succinctly abbreviated to the acronym 'Q-KOB'.

Making use of acronyms is harnessing the 'freak-out' principle to assist in the memorisation process. Where the acronym gives a good indication of the bidding structure to be learnt, maximum efficiency is produced. 'Stayman', 'Flannery', 'South African Texas' etc do little to assist the learning of the conventions involved. By contrast, the acronym CRASH serves as its own memory guide for the conventional approach it represents. C-RA-SH stands for 'colour, rank, shape' the order in which suits are shown in, for example, Roman Blackwood (5♡ = 2 aces same colour, 5♠ = 2 aces, same rank, 5NT two suits same shape—hearts and clubs, rounded, *or* spades and diamonds, pointed), a defence against strong 1♣ openings or Forcing Pass systems or over their 1NT opening (e.g. after they open 1NT, 2♣ = 2 suits of the same colour, 2◇ = 2 suits of the same rank, 2NT = 2 suits of the same shape) or in a system of two-suited two-openings where 2♡ = 2 suits of the same colour; 2♠ = 2 suits of the same rank and 2NT = 2 suits of the same shape. If this approach is used in several areas of the system, obviously it is best to keep the order of the suits the same in each area.

Suppose that you preferred to have a different order of the suits for two-suiters. For example, suppose that you wished the order to be rank, colour, shape. You should try to create a mnemonic which will make the order simple to recall. If one of the members of your partnership has a name that lends itself to this exercise, so much the better. For instance, if one of the names happens to be 'Richard', a suitable mnemonic would be RCO = **R**ichard **C**an **O**perate = **R**ank, **C**olour, **O**dd. If the order that was considered best was rank, shape, colour, then a suitable mnemonic might be **R**eady **M**ixed **C**oncrete = RMC = **R**ank, **M**ixed, **C**olour.

Suppose that in your big club system, you are able to determine by a 2♠ bid from partner that the hand pattern held was 4-4-3-2. You could then enquire with 2NT for the two suits held. Would you consider this a suitable scheme?

2NT enquiry: 3 ♣ = clubs and diamonds *or* clubs and hearts (3♦ then
relays and 3♥ = clubs and hearts, 3♠ = clubs
and diamonds)
3 ♦ = diamonds and hearts
3 ♥ = hearts and spades
3 ♠ = spades and clubs
3NT = spades and diamonds

This is clearly an awkward structure with there being no relation between 3♣ showing two combinations and 3♦/3♥/3♠ showing the suit bid and the next suit along and 3NT showing the missing combination. A simpler guide would be: 'Over 2NT bid the cheaper four-card suit. If necessary, partner relays for the second suit.' This is no more than bidding the four-card suits up-the-line so that the scheme becomes:

2NT enquiry: 3 ♣ = clubs and a higher suit (3 ♦ relays and in reply,
3 ♥ = hearts, 3 ♠ = spades, 3NT = diamonds,
the relay suit)
3 ♦ = diamonds and a higher suit (3 ♥ relays and in
reply, 3 ♠ = spades and 3NT = hearts, the relay
suit)
3 ♥ = hearts and spades

All that one needs to remember in this approach is the up-the-line rule.

Note that after the relay, suits are shown genuinely (3 ♥ = hearts, etc) and this is also a distinct advantage to simplify both the learning and the memorisation. Suppose partner opens 1♥ and you are using 2♦ as a game forcing relay. You could have opener continue by bidding 2♠ to show a balanced hand and 2NT to show a heart-spade two-suiter or by bidding 2♠ to show the spade-heart two-suiter and 2NT to show the balanced variety. You would need to have highly compelling reasons not to select the latter, natural approach.

In some cases you may wish deliberately to avoid the natural meaning of a bid. Suppose that you and partner wished to use splinters over a major suit opening but you believed that natural splinters 1-Major: 4♣ to show a club shortage or 1-Major: 4♦ to show a diamond shortage gave the opposition too much leeway to double to suggest a sacrifice. Which of these two alternative structures would you prefer to adopt where responder is promising support and a splinter-type hand?

(i)		(ii)	
1♠ : 3NT	= a void somewhere	1♠ : 3NT	= a void somewhere
1♡ : 3♠	= a void somewhere	1♡ : 3♠	= a void somewhere
1♠ : 4♣	= a heart singleton	1♠ : 4♣	= a heart singleton
1♠ : 4♢	= a club singleton	1♠ : 4♢	= a diamond singleton
1♠ : 4♡	= a diamond singleton	1♠ : 4♡	= a club singleton
1♡ : 3NT	= a spade singleton	1♡ : 3NT	= a spade singleton
1♡ : 4♣	= a diamond singleton	1♡ : 4♣	= a diamond singleton
1♡ : 4♢	= club singleton	1♡ : 4♢	= a club singleton

After 1♠ : 3NT, 4♣ is a relay and
    4♢ = heart void
    4♡ = diamond void
    4♠ = club void

After 1♡ : 3♠, 3NT is the relay and
    4♣ = spade void
    4♢ = club void
    4♡ = diamond void

After 1♠ : 3NT, 4♣ is a relay and
    4♢ = heart void
    4♡ = diamond void
    4♠ = club void

After 1♡ : 3♠, 3NT is the relay and
    4♣ = spade void
    4♢ = diamond void
    4♡ = club void

The two structures are similar. Structure (ii) follows the principle that the short suit is shown in rank order: spades/hearts/diamond/clubs and this order is kept constant throughout. Structure (i) follows the same principle but breaks the pattern when the bid would show the natural suit. Thus instead of 4♢ showing a diamond singleton in 1♠ : 4♢, this is deliberately changed so that no bids are natural. Structure (ii) is definitely preferred for the sake of memory, because there is a constant thread that applies to each of the bids. If it is considered desirable to avoid bidding the natural shortage, then a different principle should be adopted, for example, by bidding the suit 'below' the shortage. Thus 1♠ : 4♣/4♢/4♡ would show a diamond/heart/club singleton.

Incidentally it is highly dangerous to use a natural-sounding bid for an artificial purpose. 1♠ : 4♡ as a splinter is such a dangerous usage and more than one player has in the heat of battle forgotten the splinter and passed partner in 4♡ for a never-to-be-forgotten result! For the same reason, 1NT : 4♡ as a transfer to spades is a risky convention and this sequence has been forgotten at the World Teams Olympiad level. Most players who wish to use transfers at the four-level prefer to use the harder-to-forget South African Texas Transfers of 1NT : 4♣ = transfer to hearts and 1NT : 4♢ = transfer to spades.

When playing four-suit-transfers over 1NT, two schemes are common:

    (i) 1NT : 2♣ = Stayman
             2◇ = transfer to hearts
             2♡ = transfer to spades
             2♠ = transfer to clubs
          2NT = natural, invitational
             3♣ = transfer to diamonds

    (ii) 1NT : 2♣ = Stayman
             2◇ = transfer to hearts
             2♡ = transfer to spades
             2♠ = transfer to clubs
          2NT = transfer to diamonds
      (invitational hands use 1NT : 2♣)
       All 3-level bids are natural

The drawback to the first method is that one of the transfer bids occurs at the three-level. The drawback to the second method is that 1NT : 2NT is a natural sequence which is very easy to forget. However, it has the advantage for memory's sake that all 2-level replies are artificial while all 3-level bids are natural. 1NT : 2NT as a transfer to diamonds has a theoretical benefit (allowing opener to bid 3♣ to show a good fit for diamonds) but has a theoretical loss in that 2♣ is required for invitational hands, which may give the defence helpful information. Of the two, we would opt for method (ii), but it is a close decision.

Relay systems are all the rage these days and these systems are proliferating at an alarming rate. The most successful will be those which are relatively easy to learn and memorise, either because they make frequent use of natural bids or because they contain principles which apply again and again throughout the system. At present the most successful of these kinds of relay systems are the 'symmetric' relays developed by Roy Kerr of New Zealand and Paul Marston, formerly of New Zealand but now of Australia. These systems have a structure whereby the shapes of hands are always resolved the same way. No matter which suit is opened, no matter which is the long suit, when it comes to showing the hand pattern, the method is regularly the same. This means that only one body of learning is required and once that has been acquired, it can be applied in all the other relevant areas.

One such principle which can be helpful is 'high-shortage-first'. This can then be utilised in every situation where the rest of the shape is being described. For example, suppose that 1♣ : 2♠ shows some 4–4–4–1 pattern, 2NT enquires and the singleton is then shown in rank order: 3♣ = spade singleton, 3♦ = heart singleton, 3♥ = diamond singleton, 3♠ = club singleton . . . the high singleton coming first. Likewise, suppose that after 1NT : 2♦ (game-force relay), opener bids 3♣ to show a 4–4–3–2 with both minors. Over the next relay of 3♦, 3♥ would show a doubleton spade (2–3–4–4) and 3♠ would show a doubleton heart (3–2–4–4), using the high-shortage-first rule. Again, if opener has rebid 2NT after 1♥ : 2♦ (game-force relay) to show a 5–3–3–2 shape with five hearts, then over the next relay of 3♣, opener would show the doubleton in the same manner (3♦ = spade doubleton, 2–5–3–3; 3♥ = diamond doubleton, 3–5–2–3; 3♠ = club doubleton, 3–5–3–2). All shortages can be resolved the same way so that when the situation arises at the table and there is a temporary mental block as to the correct shape-showing bid, there is a convenient rule which can be applied and the correct reply can be calculated from first principles.

(2) Learning The System

It is generally accepted that the expert can perpetrate greater horrors than the novice not through lack of ability but by forgetfulness. The disasters which follow from forgetting a transfer far exceed those which follow from the novice's failure to count trumps. There are techniques which will speed up the learning process and while individual learning methods differ greatly, the following will usually produce the best results.

It is possible to learn the outline of a complex system within 2–3 weeks. It normally takes a year or so to feel completely comfortable with the system and to know how to utilise the tools that it provides. Learning how the system operates is the easy part; learning how to operate the system is what leads to ultimate success.

(a) Organise the system materials in small doses rather than in large ones It is preferable to have the system summarised on a hundred small cards than on twenty foolscap pages. When reading and re-reading these summaries, the smaller cards make use of the 'first-in, last-out' principles, since you will start a card and finish a card more often than a large sheet of close-typed material. Smaller cards also appear far less daunting than large expanses of type.

(b) Space your system-learning sessions into frequent short sessions rather than fewer long sessions Six one-hour sessions will produce far better results than two three-hour sessions. Again this makes best use of the 'first-in, last-out' principles.

(c) Highlight special system areas with coloured marker pens This will heighten their impact through the 'freak-out' principle. Give unusual names to unusual conventions within the system for the same purpose, either acronyms or mnemonics which will make them easier to recall.

(d) Cross-reference system areas in which the same principles apply This will allow the effect of the 'close-encounters' principle to operate.

(e) Use examples, quizzes, exercises as often as possible The partners can give each other problems or exercises regularly. Bid as many hands as possible from books, magazines or newspaper columns using your system. This repetition is far more interesting than a continual reading of dull system notes. If you have access to a computer which can generate specific hand types (not too tough these days), arrange to have hands for each system area produced and then practise bidding them with your partner. If you have troubles meeting regularly with your partner, each of you should bid the hands and later compare your auctions. Repetition is the most effective long-term memory tool.

(f) Institute a system of fines when either partner forgets a system bid This will operate as part of the 'freakout' principle since forgotten bids which involve some kind of fine will be well remembered the next time the situation arises. As the story goes, Terence Reese and Boris Schapiro had a system of £1 fines when either of them forgot a transfer sequence. Money collected from fines should be put into something like lottery tickets from which both partners share the proceeds.

It may be desirable to have a scale of fines, agreed in advance, with more serious lapses being more heavily fined. In this era of Forcing Pass systems, it is not uncommon for a player who has recently adopted such a system forgetting the meaning of 'Pass' and passing when a bid should have been made or bidding when 'Pass' indicated the strength held. A light-hearted recent incident saw a nouveau Forcing Passer passing in fourth seat in a situation where a bid was essential since partner's earlier 'Pass' was unlimited. The upshot was a missed slam and when scoring up came and their teammates read out 'Board 8. 6♣, −920' their 'Board 8. Passed in. Minus 14 Imps.' was greeted with 'Passed in? Passed in??? How did the bidding go??'

Until such a radical system is firmly entrenched it is a wise move to say to yourself before each hand begins, 'Remember, I'm playing Forcing Pass . . .' or whatever.

(g) Avoid as far as possible playing other methods while you are learning a new system If you wish to play a complex system and you wish to play it well, it will take a commitment from you and partner to stick with the system and

with each other for at least a year. To play conflicting methods in this time will make life tough for the partnership, since this works counter to the 'close-encounters' principle. Do not be dismayed if your results at an early stage of a new system are poorish. This is normal since so much of your energies are caught up in recalling the system that you cannot devote sufficient attention to leads, declarer play and defence and plays that would normally not elude you may well slip past your guard at this stage. However, these will all be restored to their former standard once the system is fully understood and has become second nature to you.

(h) Even after the system has been fully learnt and is fully operational, spend some time every year (say two to three times a year), going through your materials again There is no substitute for the 'play-it-again-and-again-Sam' principle. If you go through your notes twenty times, you will be better equipped than if you have gone through them only a dozen times. This still applies after you have full confidence with the system. Some small area might easily slip under your guard. Regular revisions will be duly rewarded by the absence of embarrassing memory lapses.

(B) MEMORY PROBLEMS IN THE PLAY

The fact that you have reached an advanced or expert level indicates that you have few problems in memory requirements for top play. Nevertheless, it is very easy to become negligent and we have seen top class players forget that a trump was still out, miss an obvious nine tricks in Three No-Trumps, fail to realise that a certain card is a winner and so on. From time to time you will have to force yourself to pay closer attention to the cards played. It is so easy to miss a key card by failing to look at the cards played (the writer has been guilty of such a lapse in the World Teams Olympiad and muffed an easy vulnerable game as a result of having failed to see the actual cards played).

You can improve your concentration and your faculty of recall by following the recommended patterns of behaviour during top class tournaments:

(a) No liquor for the duration of the tournament. Players who believe that alcohol does not affect their performances are fooling only themselves. Some inexplicable play or bid in the session following a few drinks will invariably arise. The effect of alcohol can last for twenty-four hours. Just because you have the evening session off that does not mean you are free to drink, thinking all will be well for the morning session since you have the night to sleep it off.

[72]

Let the other guys drink during the tournament and they can join you for drinks when celebrating your victory.

(b) Avoid eating immediately prior to a session. Heavy meals play havoc with your ability to concentrate and with your memory. Try to finish meals at least one hour before play commences. If this is impossible, make it only the lightest of snacks.

(c) Try to have plenty of sleep during a major tournament. You can congratulate the disco brigade who bridge all day and party all night on their stamina while they are congratulating you on your win.

(d) Try to achieve at least a minimal degree of fitness before a major tournament. Your performance will improve, both as to concentration and endurance, as fitness improves. Major championships are generally held over one to two weeks. Much of your time is spent in smoke-laden atmospheres. Can you afford to give an edge to those competitors who are not as bright as you are but who perform better because they are fitter? Between sessions it will also assist you if you can catch a few minutes of fresh air, have a shower or a change of attire to freshen yourself.

THE PHENOMENON OF PRESSURE

Players will often make unaccountable errors, plays which they can scarcely believe they have made, because of the existence of 'pressure', a very real phenomenon at all levels of play. Pressure can cause physical manifestations such as hands shaking, feet trembling, facial tics, and the like. Very few major tournaments are won by players making their first appearance, partly because they are not accustomed to the pressure that is involved. Experience (having been there before often) is one of the best means of coping with pressure. A sympathetic partner is of invaluable assistance (an unsympathetic partner will add to the pressure) and simply being aware of the existence of pressure will reduce its effect on your play.

TIPS FOR THE PLAY

(1) Be familiar with all your defensive methods, whether it is leads, signals or discards. If you can align your methods so that you are doing the same thing in many situations, that will ease your memory worries. For example, reverse signals (lowest to encourage, high-low to discourage) are not merely technically superior. They also allow you to play the same cards in the trump suit as in other suits (reverse signallers when giving count play the lowest from an even number of cards, peter with a odd number). If you are also

using attitude leads rather than the standard fourth-highest, this dovetails neatly with reverse signals since with attitude leads, the lowest card is encouraging and a high-card-lead indicates little interest in the suit.

(2) Giving the opposition memory problems

We have already seen that 'red on red, black on black' and a key discard when an opponent is least likely to be attentive can lead him to errors later in the play. Likewise when there is no other prospect, one may as well lead out all one's trumps and outside winners and hope that an opponent makes an error in discarding. One is regularly rewarded for these cost-nothing plays. You will often notice that a top player, when playing for such an error, plays the cards as quickly as possible. The quicker the player, the less chance the opponents have to keep up with what is going on. With many experts it is safe to conclude that the quicker the tempo, the more desperate the contract.

The corollary is that you should never allow declarer to dictate the pace of play. Play at your own pace, deliberately slow down the tempo if you believe declarer is engaging in this tactic and ignore signs of impatience from an opponent. Force yourself to look at every card played and do not turn over your own card until you are satisfied you are aware of what is happening. Be prepared to take time out to make whatever calculations you need for your own play.

We have also seen that when you are defending it may pay you to discard early on from a suit that you know is breaking 3–3. If declarer misses the discard, he may not realise that the suit has divided evenly and may neglect to cash a card that is in fact a winner.

(3) The Memory Coup

There is a certain kind of play that is based on an opponent's being uncertain of which is your last card. How many times has it happened that the wrong card is discarded at trick twelve? Make sure you do not face your last card until the opponents have completed their play to the twelfth trick. A premature revelation of your last card may allow an opponent to recover when the wrong card might have been retained.

There is a certain art in being able to induce this kind of error. See how you would handle the defence of this hand, playing pairs where every overtrick is critical:

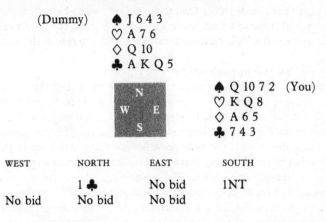

(Dummy)   ♠ J 6 4 3
     ♡ A 7 6
     ◇ Q 10
     ♣ A K Q 5

           ♠ Q 10 7 2   (You)
           ♡ K Q 8
           ◇ A 6 5
           ♣ 7 4 3

WEST	NORTH	EAST	SOUTH
	1 ♣	No bid	1NT
No bid	No bid	No bid	

West leads the ◇ 2 to your ace. You return a diamond and West wins the king. ◇ J from West takes the third trick, dummy discarding a heart, and West's ◇ 9 wins trick four, dummy discarding a low spade, you discard a sly club and declarer follows with the ◇ 8. West switches to the ♡ 10, denying the jack, ducked to your queen. Your ♡ 8 dislodges dummy's ace and declarer plays off the ♣ AK, dropping the jack and 10 from hand as West follows with the 8 and 2. The ace and king of spades are played, leading to this endposition:

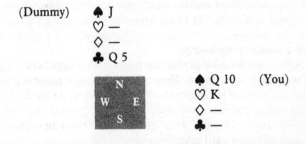

(Dummy)   ♠ J
     ♡ —
     ◇ —
     ♣ Q 5

           ♠ Q 10   (You)
           ♡ K
           ◇ —
           ♣ —

Now, do *not* look back at the description of play above . . . South leads the ♣ 9 to dummy's queen on which you discard the ♠ 10. Finally, the ♣ 5 is led . . . Which major suit winner do you retain? You know that declarer has the ♡ J left as well as one club, but which club is it? If the lead stays in dummy, you must retain the ♠ Q but if declarer will win the club trick, you must discard your ♠ Q and cling to the king of hearts. Make your decision before consulting the complete hand:

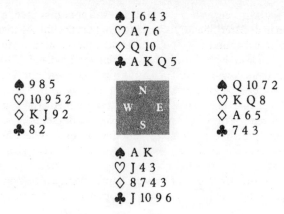

```
                        ♠ J 6 4 3
                        ♡ A 7 6
                        ◇ Q 10
                        ♣ A K Q 5
  ♠ 9 8 5                              ♠ Q 10 7 2
  ♡ 10 9 5 2          N               ♡ K Q 8
  ◇ K J 9 2       W       E           ◇ A 6 5
  ♣ 8 2               S               ♣ 7 4 3
                        ♠ A K
                        ♡ J 4 3
                        ◇ 8 7 4 3
                        ♣ J 10 9 6
```

Declarer always had seven tricks and unless the ♠ Q fell short, there were no real chances for eight tricks. However, declarer skilfully played on the failure of almost every defender to pay attention to the 'insignificant' pips in the irrelevant suit, clubs in this case. Almost invariably, by the time East recognises the problem, the spots held and played in clubs have faded from memory and the defender is left with an unenviable guess. Note that declarer's play of the clubs, dropping the jack and ten under the ace-king, was without risk, since if the clubs did not split, declarer still had the queen and nine as winners.

At the table when you are a defender faced with this kind of play, sit up and take notice when declarer starts unblocking high cards. If you pay attention to the pips at that moment, you will be well-placed to know which card to retain in the ending.

Quite often declarer will be able to use this manoeuvre without having to do any significant unblocking at all. If the layout looks like this:

> Dummy: Q 6 4 3
> Declarer: A K 7 2

declarer has no prospects for an extra trick if the suit does not break 3–2, but if it divides normally, declarer can generate a memory coup and can organise the play to have the fourth round of the suit won in either hand. After the ace and king have been played, confirming that the suit does divide 3–2, declarer can lead the 7 to the queen or the 2 to the queen. If declarer wants to have the lead remain in dummy, best is to pitch the 6 and 4 under the ace and king and lead the 7 to the queen. When the 3 is led, it will appear as though the trick will be won in declarer's hand. In order to heighten the illusion that dummy will win the fourth round, play the 3 and 4 under the ace-king, retaining the 6 in dummy, but lead the 2 to the queen, keeping the 7 in hand. When the 6 is led, most defenders will consider that the 6 will keep the lead in dummy if they have not been attentive in the earlier play.

If possible, it is an idea to play off the first two rounds of this suit earlier in the play. Then when the third round is played towards the end, you will have the 'last-out' principle working in your favour since other things have elapsed between the significant early plays and the critical moment of decision.

Even if it is patently obvious where the fourth round will be won, you may still be able to engineer the play so that an opponent is uncertain of what is going on.

Dummy: Q 4 3 2
Declarer: A K 10 9

Here, declarer cannot avoid winning the fourth round of the suit if the ace, king and queen have been played. However, if declarer can manage to discard the 9 earlier in the play (after checking out the suit division) and right-hand opponent misses this discard, you may be able to pull off this ploy again. For example, cash the ace and lead the 10 to the queen, lead winners from dummy on which you discard the 9 at some unobtrusive moment. Later return to your king and at the end of the hand, cross to a winner in dummy and lead the 2, 3 or 4 whichever you have left at trick twelve. Your right-hand opponent will have to be sharp to be sure where this trick will be taken.

Obviously these plays work only when the lead at trick twelve comes from dummy and it is only your right-hand opponent who can be fooled. When the opportunity for this manoeuvre does not exist, you should arrange your play to make sure you win the twelfth trick in hand. Clearly if dummy wins trick twelve, no one will have any problem in deciding what to keep. If you win the trick in your own hand at trick twelve, both opponents may be hard-pressed to be certain of your thirteenth card.

The following deals all feature 'memory coups' which succeeded at the table. Perhaps the opposition should have done better but that does not detract from the plays themselves.

Dealer West
Nil vulnerable

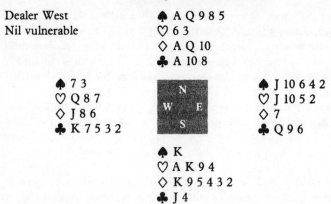

♠ A Q 9 8 5
♡ 6 3
◇ A Q 10
♣ A 10 8

♠ 7 3
♡ Q 8 7
◇ J 8 6
♣ K 7 5 3 2

♠ J 10 6 4 2
♡ J 10 5 2
◇ 7
♣ Q 9 6

♠ K
♡ A K 9 4
◇ K 9 5 4 3 2
♣ J 4

North opened 1♠ and after a series of artificial relays, South became declarer in 7◇ without having revealed any aspect of the shape of the South hand. North's shape and controls had been disclosed to the opposition and West led the ♣ 3. Declarer took the ♣ A and dropped a cost-nothing ♣ J from hand. A spade went to the king, a diamond back to the ace and a low spade was ruffed. Next came the king of diamonds—had diamonds been 2–2, the hand would have been over—on which East discarded a club. A diamond to dummy's queen drew West's last trump and East let go the ♣ Q, since he could not spare a spade and was not sure of the heart position. Declarer played off the ♠ AQ, discarding two hearts, ruffed a spade to hand and with four cards remaining played off the last diamond. West was down to ♡ Q-8-7 and the ♣ K and was now regretting not having paid closer attention to the clubs that had been discarded earlier. Finally, the ♣ K was discarded in order not to unguard the queen of hearts and declarer's ♣ 4 won the thirteenth trick.

This next deal saw the defenders put declarer to a guess:

Advanced to Expert Techniques

Dealer East
North-South vulnerable

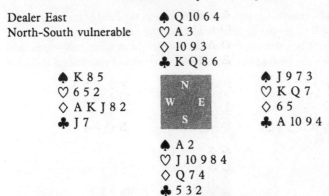

♠ Q 10 6 4
♡ A 3
◇ 10 9 3
♣ K Q 8 6

♠ K 8 5
♡ 6 5 2
◇ A K J 8 2
♣ J 7

♠ J 9 7 3
♡ K Q 7
◇ 6 5
♣ A 10 9 4

♠ A 2
♡ J 10 9 8 4
◇ Q 7 4
♣ 5 3 2

Playing pairs, West opened 1NT (12–14 points) in third seat and this was passed out. North decided to try for a 'safe' lead with the ◇ 10 and West promptly reeled off five rounds of diamonds. On the fourth round, North pitched the ♡ 3 first and then the ♣ 6, dummy let go two spades and a club, and South discarded ♡ J and the ♣ 2. Declarer now led the ♣ J–Q–A and the ♣ 10 was taken by North's king. A low spade was won by South and West's ♠ K won the spade return, leaving this position:

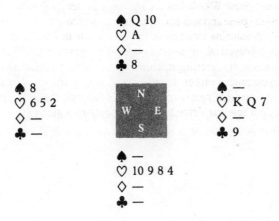

♠ Q 10
♡ A
◇ —
♣ 8

♠ 8
♡ 6 5 2
◇ —
♣ —

♠ —
♡ K Q 7
◇ —
♣ 9

♠ —
♡ 10 9 8 4
◇ —
♣ —

West led a heart taken by the ace. On the ♠ Q, dummy let go a top heart but when the ♠ 10 was played, declarer was unable to tell whether North held a club or a heart and wrongly elected to throw the ♣ 9 from dummy, holding the contract to just seven tricks.

[79]

The final offering is the pièce-de-résistance in the field of memory coups, a rare example of genius in defence as East converts defeat into a chance of success by neatly sidestepping declarer's attempt at a stepping-stone and thereby suddenly gaining the upper hand. How would you defend as East in this situation:

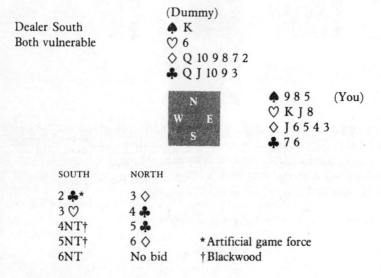

(Dummy)
♠ K
♡ 6
♦ Q 10 9 8 7 2
♣ Q J 10 9 3

Dealer South
Both vulnerable

♠ 9 8 5   (You)
♡ K J 8
♦ J 6 5 4 3
♣ 7 6

SOUTH	NORTH	
2 ♣*	3 ♦	
3 ♡	4 ♣	
4 NT†	5 ♣	
5 NT†	6 ♦	*Artificial game force
6 NT	No bid	†Blackwood

West led the ♡ 10. Which card should East play?

Suppose that South won the first trick and continued with the A–K of clubs, followed by the ♦ A on which West showed out, discarding the ♠ 2. On the ♦ K, West discarded another spade. A spade went to the king and dummy's three clubs were cashed. What should East discard?

Make your decision before consulting the complete deal:

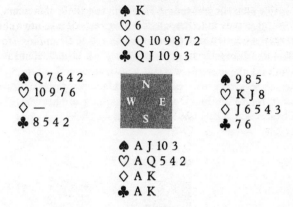

Had West led a spade, that would have curtailed the play promptly, but the spade lead was not necessarily safe. On the ♡ 10, East followed with the jack, taken by the queen. South cashed the four minor suit winners and crossed to the ♠ K. On dummy's three club winners East let go two spades and the *king* of hearts. This was the end-position:

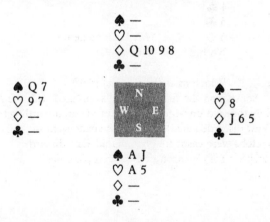

The queen of diamonds was led, South discarding the ♡5 and West discarding the ♡7. Then came the ◇ 10 and while East paused for thought, declarer gave a sign of impatience, as if to claim. East knew that South must have both major aces left and thus if East won the ♢ 10, that would be the end of proceedings: if he led a diamond, dummy would take the rest while if he led the heart, declarer would take the two aces. *East let dummy's ♢ 10 hold the trick*. Declarer discarded the ♠ J and West let go the ♠ 7. When East won the next diamond, the pressure was suddenly transferred to South who had to decide which major ace to keep. Now East's farsighted play in hearts came home to roost, for South finally, after much sighing and heaving, discarded the ace of hearts and East's ♡ 8 was the setting trick!

Appendix I

FROM WHIST TO BRIDGE

GAME 1—NO-TRUMPS WHIST

Each player receives 13 cards. Opposite players are partners. There is no bidding yet. The player on the left of the dealer makes the first lead, that is, places one card face up on the table. Each player plays a card face up in turn in clockwise order. That group of four cards, one from each player, is called a *trick*. A trick is won by the highest card of the suit led. *Each player must follow suit if possible*. If you are unable to follow suit, you should discard those cards which you judge to be worthless.

A trick can be won only by a card in the same suit as the card led. That holds true in all cases except when there is a trump suit (see next game). You may play a high card or a low card but if possible, you must follow suit. One situation where you could win the trick but it could be foolish to do so is if you are last to play to a trick and partner's card has already won the trick.

Play continues until all 13 tricks have been played and each side then counts up the number of tricks won. The side winning more than 6 tricks is the winner and is the only side that scores points.

Scoring
The first partnership to score **100 points or more** in tricks won scores a GAME. We play a RUBBER of bridge and a rubber is **best of three games**. The first partnership to win two games wins the rubber. A 2–0 win scores 700 bonus points, a 2–1 wins scores 500 bonus points.

The trick score in No-Trumps is:
30 points for each trick won over six, plus 10.

So 7 tricks (making 1NT) is worth 40 points, 8 tricks (2NT) is worth 70, 9 tricks (3NT) is worth 100, and so on.

Appendix I

A bridge scoresheet looks like this:

Trick scores are written below the line, bonus scores are written above the line. At the end of a game, a line is ruled across both columns and both sides start the next game from zero again. At the end of a rubber the scores in each column are tallied and the higher scoring side is the winner. The difference between the two scores is rounded off to the nearest 100 (e.g. 870 goes to 900, 820 goes to 800, and 850 also goes down to 800) and the score is entered as the number of 100s won or lost. For example, if you won by 900, your scoresheet reads '+9' while their scoresheet would record '—9'.

Guidelines for play at no-trumps

Prefer to lead your longest suit and keep on with that suit. When the others run out, your remaining cards in that suit will be winners, since they cannot win the trick if they cannot follow suit. As players lead their own long suit, prefer to return partner's led suit, unless you have a strong suit of your own, and usually avoid returning a suit led by the opposition.

Second player to a trick commonly plays low, third player to a trick commonly plays high. If partner's card has already won the trick, you need not beat partner's card in fourth seat.

The card to lead: Top card from a sequence of three or more cards headed by the ten or higher (e.g. from K-Q-J-5, lead the K; from J-10-9-8, lead the J).

Lead fourth-highest (fourth from the top) where the long suit has no three-card or longer sequence. (e.g. from K-J-8-4-3, lead the 4).

After three or four games of No-Trumps Whist, move on to —

GAME 2—TRUMPS WHIST

Each player receives 13 cards. The top card of the other pack is turned up as *the trump suit*. There is still no bidding. The player on the left of dealer leads the first card and each player MUST FOLLOW SUIT if possible.

Tricks without a trump card are won by the highest card of the suit led; tricks with a trump card are won by the highest trump card.

If you cannot follow suit, you may trump in but are not forced to do so. If partner has won the trick, it is usually poor tactics to trump partner's winner.

Scoring
With SPADES or HEARTS as trumps: 30 points for each trick over six.
With DIAMONDS or CLUBS as trumps: 20 points for each trick over six.

Guidelines for play at trumps
Leading the longest suit is no longer so attractive. Prefer to lead a strong suit (headed by a *sequence* or by A–K) or a singleton (so you can trump in). Leading out aces or doubleton honours is not appealing. With plenty of trumps, lead trumps to remove the opponents' trump cards so that they cannot trump your winners. If you lead a doubleton (two cards in the suit), standard technique is to lead top card from a doubleton.

After three or four games of Trumps Whist, move on to —

GAME 3—DUMMY WHIST

Each player receives 13 cards. *The partner of the dealer puts all 13 cards face up in suits on the table* (the DUMMY hand). DECLARER (partner of the DUMMY) then states the trump suit or no-trumps.

To choose a trump suit, the suit should have 8 or more cards in the combined hands; if more than one trump suit is available, choose a major suit (hearts or spades) rather than a minor suit (clubs or diamonds) as the majors score more; if the suits are both majors or both minors, choose the longer or if both have the same length, choose the stronger. If there is no suit with 8 or more trumps together, usually prefer to play no-trumps.

After the trump suit or no-trumps has been stated, the player on the left of the declarer makes the first lead. The play proceeds as before but DECLARER MUST PLAY BOTH HANDS. The Dummy player takes no part in the play. If dummy wins a trick, the next lead comes from dummy.

Scoring
As above.

The existence of the DUMMY hand marks off Bridge games from other trick-taking games like Five Hundred, Solo and Whist. From the first lead, each player can see half the pack (13 cards in hand plus 13 cards in dummy), thus making Bridge essentially a game of skill, in contrast to the large luck factor in the other games.

Play at least four hands of Dummy Whist before proceeding to —

GAME 4—BIDDING WHIST (COUNTING POINTS)

Each player receives 13 cards. Each player totals the high card points in hand according to A = 4, K = 3, Q = 2, J = 1. Starting with the dealer, each player states how many points are held. There are 40 HCP in the pack, 10 in each suit. The side with the higher number of points becomes the declarer side and the two partners discuss which suit shall be trumps or whether to play no-trumps. Each partner names a possible trump suit or no-trumps in turn, until agreement is reached. To suggest a trump suit, the suit should contain five or more cards, or at the very least four. With no particularly long suit and no void (void means no cards in a suit) and no singleton (a singleton is just one card in a suit), it is usually best to suggest no-trumps straight away. If there is no early agreement and neither partner insists on a suit, one should suggest no-trumps. After agreement is reached the first player to suggest that suit or no-trumps becomes the declarer. If both sides have 20 points, the player with the most points and partner do the bidding. If still equal, deal a new hand.

In the play, the player *on the left of the declarer* makes the opening lead *before seeing dummy*. After the lead, the 13 dummy cards are placed face up (in suits), facing declarer. Trumps go on dummy's right.

Scoring

As above, but if declarer fails to win seven tricks, the opposition (the defenders) score 50 points for each trick by which declarer has failed, regardless of whether the contract is no-trumps, spades, hearts, diamonds or clubs. For example, if declarer takes five tricks, the defenders score 100 points. Defenders' points go above the line as *bonuses*. *Only the declarer side can score points for game*. This 50 per trick increases to 100 per trick if declarer is "vulnerable".

Vulnerable = Having won one game

Not vulnerable = Not having won a game yet

Play as many games of BIDDING WHIST as time allows.

ADDITIONAL MATERIAL

If you have extra time available, (perhaps more than one introductory lesson
or you are teaching schoolchildren and there is no limit on the number of
classes, etc.), there are a few extra games that can be played. The above are
the best for just one lesson but the following are also fun to play.

GAME 2A—DEALER'S WHIST—USE AFTER GAME 2

Each player receives 13 cards. The dealer, after examining the 13 cards held
and without consulting partner, names the trump suit or no-trumps. This
gives the dealer some control over the trump position, whereas in Game 2,
the card turned up as trumps is purely a matter of luck.

Tip: Choose as your trump suit only a suit with five or more cards. With
no five-card suit, usually prefer no-trumps.

Play
As for Games 1 and 2. There is no dummy.

Scoring
As for Games 1 and 2.

GAME 3A—PARTNERSHIP WHIST—AFTER GAME 3

Each player receives 13 cards. The dealer and dealer's partner discuss
whether to play in trumps or no-trumps. Each suggests no-trumps or a
trump suit in turn. If no trump suit is agreed after three turns each, the play
is at no-trumps with the dealer as declarer. If a trump suit or no-trumps is
agreed earlier, the player suggesting that suit first (or NT first) is declarer.

Play
The opening lead is made by the player on declarer's left. Dummy's cards
are not turned face up until after the opening lead is made.

Scoring
As for Games 1 and 2.

Appendix I

GAME 4A—CONTRACT WHIST WITH BIDDING—USE AFTER GAME 4

The early play proceeds exactly as GAME 4—BIDDING WHIST. However, instead of needing to win just 7 or more tricks, the declarer is required to win a specific number of tricks depending on the total number of points held by declarer and dummy:

20–22 points:	7 or more tricks in no-trumps
	8 or more tricks with a trump suit
23–25 points:	8 or more tricks in no-trumps
	9 or more tricks with a trump suit
26–32 points:	9 or more tricks in no-trumps
	10 or more tricks with hearts or spades as trumps
	11 or more tricks with clubs or diamonds as trumps
33–36 points:	12 or more tricks
37–40 points:	All 13 tricks

Play

The player on declarer's left leads before dummy appears.

Scoring

The same as for GAME 4—BIDDING WHIST, but to score points declarer must win the number of tricks stipulated or more. If declarer wins less than the stipulated number, the defenders score bonus points (above the line) of 50 or 100 for each trick by which declarer fails (50 per trick if declarer is not vulnerable, 100 per trick if vulnerable).

If declarer is required to win 12 tricks ('small slam') and does so, the declarer side scores an extra bonus of 500 if not vulnerable or 750 if vulnerable. If declarer is required to win all 13 tricks ('grand slam') and does so, the declarer side scores an extra 1000 if not vulnerable or 1500 if vulnerable.

Appendix II

SOLUTION TO EXERCISES ON SECTION TWO

1. Memory code for opener's reply to Ogust 2NT enquiry:
minors minimum, 1-2, 1-2-3
The 1-2, 1-2-3 refer to the top honours held in opener's long suit.

2. The first series of answers would be covered by the rule:
'Show the singleton in rank order: ♠/♡/◇/♣'
The second series is covered by 'bid the suit below the singleton'.

3. (a) Do not bid 2♠. South should pass. The suit is too weak. (see page 35)

(b) Do not bid 2♠. South should pass. The spade suit is too weak. (see page 35)

(c) You should not double for penalties. There are not sufficient trump winners. (see the rule of 6 and 4 on page 36)

4. (a) The spade suit is divided 5-3 or 4-4 if North's ♠ 3 lead is fourth highest. The odds are that it is a 5-3 split.

(b) In hearts, the critical card is the jack. When declarer plays hearts, ♡ Q, heart to the ace and then ♡ K, you need watch for only the ♡ J.

In diamonds, the critical cards are the jack and ten. When declarer plays the ◇ A, a diamond to the king and the ◇ Q, you need watch for only the ◇ J and 10. The jack and ten might fall doubleton or if the suit divides 3-3, the jack and ten will have fallen by the third round. (see pages 39/40)

(c) With one suit wide open, and eight top winners available, declarer should tackle first the suits which do not give up the lead. After ♠ K, try the diamonds. If the diamonds do not yield the ninth trick, tackle the hearts, queen first. If the jack of hearts fails to appear, take the club finesse as the last chance.

5. (a) If West has played 5–2 in hearts on the first two tricks, thus indicating a doubleton heart, East should play a low heart at trick three, forcing West to ruff. From the appearance of dummy, it will be clear that a diamond switch is called for.

(b) If West plays 5–8 in hearts, thus indicating a third heart is held, East should continue with a third top heart. As long as declarer has only five spades, the contract might be defeated. For example, give South ♠ A Q 10 7 5 ♡ 7 4 ◇ J 6 3 ♣ 9 8 3, declarer will be able to discard one diamond on the fourth club but will still have two diamond losers and a spade loser. (see pages 44/45)

6. East must not discard any hearts (keep length with dummy—see page 47). East's last six cards should be the four hearts and the ◇ Q-J and if another spade were played, East should discard a diamond. East should deduce that if South had the ◇ K, South would have all thirteen tricks anyway. The need to hold all four hearts can be seen from the complete deal:

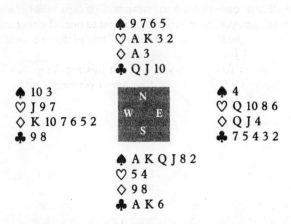

```
                    ♠ 9 7 6 5
                    ♡ A K 3 2
                    ◇ A 3
                    ♣ Q J 10
  ♠ 10 3                              ♠ 4
  ♡ J 9 7          N                  ♡ Q 10 8 6
  ◇ K 10 7 6 5 2  W   E               ◇ Q J 4
  ♣ 9 8              S                ♣ 7 5 4 3 2
                    ♠ A K Q J 8 2
                    ♡ 5 4
                    ◇ 9 8
                    ♣ A K 6
```

If at any stage before the last five tricks, East lets a heart go, South can play the ♡ A, ♡ K and ruff the third heart, setting up dummy's last heart as the thirteenth and making all the tricks. 6♠ making for North-South will be a good board for East-West since there are twelve top tricks in no-trumps, but allowing South to score the overtrick would give East-West a bottom board.

7. There will be only one trump loser on a 3–2 break about ⅔ of the time. The 4–1 break occurs about ¼ of the time. (see page 55)

8. (a) West should continue with the ♠K and a low spade, playing dummy's jack if North plays low. Because of the dangerous heart position, North must not be allowed to gain the lead and this would be a bad moment to follow 'eight ever, nine never'. North's hand is ♠ Q 6 5 ♡ Q J 8 2 ◇ A K 6 4 2 ♣ 7 and if West plays off the ♠K and ♠A without finessing, the contract can be defeated.

(b) Having already lost three heart tricks, West must play the spades the best way to try to avoid losing a spade trick. Therefore 'nine never' : ♠K and a spade to the ace. (see page 56)

9. (a) Cash the ace first. With J and 10 missing, keep two honours together. (see page 57)

(b) Cash the ace or queen first, keeping an honour card in either hand. If a 5–0 break turns up, you can restrict your losers to one. If either opponent drops the 7 or 8 on the first round, play the partner of that player as the one more likely to hold J-x-x-x.

(c) Cash the queen first. With jack and ten missing, keep two honours together. If there is a 5–0 split, you have saved yourself a trick.

10. Partner's lead of the ♠ 8, the *highest* spot card coupled with South's bidding places South with K–Q–J of spades. Even if South has K–Q–J bare, the defence will have to gain the lead on two more occasions to set the spades up and to cash them. A far better chance is to play partner to have one key card, either the ♣ K or an entry in diamonds. You should win the ♠ A at trick one and switch to clubs, selecting very carefully the *queen* of clubs as your switch, the 'surrounding' card. You have the jack surrounded, you have two cards higher than the jack. If you visualise the jack in your own hand, you would hold A–Q–J–10–9 from which the card to lead at no-trumps is the queen (see 'surround plays'—page 58). This precise defence is necessary to defeat the contract as the complete deal is:

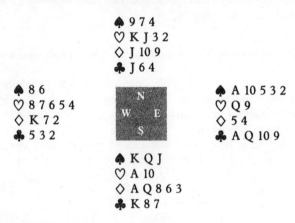

```
            ♠ 9 7 4
            ♡ K J 3 2
            ◇ J 10 9
            ♣ J 6 4

♠ 8 6                        ♠ A 10 5 3 2
♡ 8 7 6 5 4                  ♡ Q 9
◇ K 7 2                      ◇ 5 4
♣ 5 3 2                      ♣ A Q 10 9

            ♠ K Q J
            ♡ A 10
            ◇ A Q 8 6 3
            ♣ K 8 7
```

If East ducks the first spade, declarer can succeed by knocking out the king of diamonds, regardless how the defence then continues. If East wins the first spade and continues spades, it is even easier for South. If East wins the ♠ A and switches to a low club (10 or 9), declarer ducks and has a second club stopper. If East wins ♠ A and switches to ace and another club, declarer ducks and makes easily.

When East wins ♠ A and switches to the ♣ Q, South is helpless. If the ♣ K wins and a diamond goes to West's king sooner or later, a club return gives the defence three club tricks in addition to the ♠ A and ◇ K. If South ducks the ♣ Q, East continues with the 10 or 9 of clubs.

Notice that East's defence would work just as well if West had the ♣ K instead of the ◇ K.

[92]

Solution to Exercises on Section Two

When dummy holds the jack, ten or nine in a suit and partner switches to the card immediately above dummy's card, you should recognise the situation as a 'surround' play.